D0794217

Johann Beer

Twayne's World Authors Series

Ulrich Weisstein, Editor of German Literature

Indiana University

TWAS 689

IMMATURO FUN... ...ERE RAPTUS

JOHANN BEER
(1655 – 1700)

Appreciation is expressed to the
Musikbibliothek Leipzig for permission to
reproduce the portrait of Beer executed by
Peter Schenk in the year of Beer's death,
1700.

Johann Beer

By James Hardin

University of South Carolina

Twayne Publishers · Boston

Johann Beer

James Hardin

Copyright © 1983 by G. K. Hall & Company
All Rights Reserved
Published by Twayne Publishers
A Division of G. K. Hall & Company
70 Lincoln Street
Boston, Massachusetts 02111

Book Production by Marne B. Sultz
Book Design by Barbara Anderson

Printed on permanent/durable acid-free
paper and bound in the United States of
America.

Library of Congress Cataloging in Publication Data

Hardin, James N.
Johann Beer.

(Twayne's world authors series; TWAS 689)
Bibliography: 95
Includes index.
1. Beer, Johann, 1655–1700—Criticism and
interpretation. I. Title. II. Series.
PT1709.B15Z69 1983 833'.5 82-23367
ISBN 0-8057-6536-0

Contents

Chronology

(Dates of works are those of the first editions.)

1655   Beer born 28 February in St. Georgen, Austria. This is the date found in church records, although the date 28 March 1655 is found in the printed version of the sermon delivered at Beer's funeral service.

1660–1661   Attends school in St. Georgen.

1662–1665   Attends school and begins his musical education in Cloister Lambach.

1665–1669   Attends school in Cloister Reichersberg am Inn.

1669–1670   Attends the Latin school in Passau.

1670–1676   Attends the *Gymnasium poeticum* in Regensburg, and, for a few months in 1676, the University of Leipzig.

1676   Joins the orchestra of Duke August of Saxony-Weissenfels in Halle on 8 October.

1677   Publication of the first part of his novel *Der Symplicianische Weltkucker* [The Simplician World-Observer]. Part II appeared in 1678, Parts III and IV in 1679. *Der Abentheuerliche, wunderbare und unerhörte Ritter Hopffensack* [The Adventurous, Fabulous and Unheard-of Knight Hop-sack].

1678   *Printz Adimantus und der Königlichen Princessin Ormizella Liebes-Geschicht* [The Love-Story of Prince Adimantus and Princess Ormizella].

1679   Marries Rosine Elisabeth Brehmer in Halle on 17 June. *Des Abentheuerlichen Jan Rebhu Ritter Spriridon aus Perusina* [The Adventurous Jan Rebhu's Knight Spiridon of Perusina], *Des Abentheuerlichen Jan Rebhu Artlicher Pokazi I* [The Adventurous Jan Rebhu's Well-Mannered Pokazi Part I; Part II in 1680], and *Die vollkommene Comische Geschicht des Corylo I* [The Complete Comic Story of Corylo, Part I; Part II 1680].

1680   Moves to Weissenfels with his family in December. *Jucundi Jucundissimi Wunderliche Lebens-Beschreibung* [Jucundus Jucundissimus's Remarkable Life-History] and *Des berühmten Spaniers Francisci Sambelle wolausgepolirte*

Weiber-Hächel [The Well-Polished Excoriation of Women by the Famous Spaniard Francisco Sambelle].

1681 *Der neu ausgefertigte Jungfer-Hobel* [The Newly Completed Maiden's Plane], *Bestia Civitatis*, and *Der* [*sic*] *Beruhmte Narren-Spital* [The Famous Asylum of Fools].

1682 *Der politische Feuermäuer-kehrer* [The Political Chimney-Sweep], *Der politische Bratenwender* [The Political Turnspit], *Der verliebte Europeer Oder Warhafftige Liebes-Roman* [The Enamored European or True Novel of Love], and *Zendorii à Zendoriis Teutsche Winternächte Oder die ausführliche und denckwürdige Beschreibung seiner Lebens-Geschicht* [Zendorio's German Winter Nights or Detailed and Remarkable Description of His Life].

1683 *Die kurtzweiligen Sommer-Täge* [Amusing Days of Summer] and *Die Andere Ausfertigung Neu-gefangener Politischer Maul-Affen* [The Second Treatise on Newly Caught Political Fools].

1685 Named concertmaster of the Weissenfels court orchestra. *Der deutsche Kleider-Affe* [The German Who Apes French Clothing (an awkward and free translation of an impossible title)]. In this year Beer ceased publication of satirical works for twelve years.

1695 Publication of the elegiac poem *Das bittere Leyden und Sterben unsers Herren und Heylandes Jesu Christi* [The Bitter Suffering and Death of Our Lord and Savior Jesus Christ].

1697 Receives post as ducal librarian. Publication of the satirical pieces *Ursus Murmurat* and *Ursus Vulpinatur* [The Bear Growls, The Bear in Pursuit of the Fox].

1698 *Historia vom Landgraff Ludwig dem Springer* [History of Landgrave Ludwig the Jumper].

1700 Wounded 28 July during a shooting competition, dies on 6 August.

POSTHUMOUS WORKS

1700 *Der verkehrte Staats-mann* [The Deceptive Statesman] and *Der kurtzweilige Bruder Blau-Mantel* [The Amazing Brother Blue-Cloak]. The works dated 1700 may have come out in Beer's lifetime.

1701   *Bellum Musicum* [Musical War].

1704   *Der Verliebte Österreicher* [The Enamored Austrian].

1719   *Musicalische Discurse* [Musical Discourses].

Chapter One
Beer's Life

Until 1932, Johann Beer was known to the learned world as an Austrian composer and musician of the late seventeenth century, a vigorous proponent of music and the musician, a controversial figure in his own time. But in that year H. F. Menck published his dissertation, "Der Musiker im Roman" (Heidelberg, 1932), which revealed Beer's activity as a novelist, and in that same year the late Richard Alewyn completed his masterful work of scholarship and detection, *Johann Beer: Studien zum Roman des 17. Jahrhunderts*,[1] which identified over twenty satirical works by Beer that had appeared pseudonymously or anonymously. While reading the long-neglected German prose fiction of the seventeenth century, Alewyn writes in his preface, he had been taken aback by several novels that stood out fresh and vibrant in the generally arid literature of the time. Alewyn's knowledge of this little-known body of literature, his considerable deductive powers, and his keen sense for style had led him to the forgotten novels of an obscure concertmaster who is now considered by many scholars to be, next to Grimmelshausen, the most entertaining and readable novelist writing in German in the seventeenth century. And what we now know is that this man, Johann Beer—musician, composer, actor, musical theoretician, novelist—was one of the most talented and versatile figures of the time.

Alewyn reconstructed much of Beer's life on the basis of autobiographical passages in his works, archival materials, musical lexicons, general historical works, and the printed funeral oration for Beer. Considering the fact that he had relatively little substantive evidence, his biography is amazingly accurate, and were it not for an incredible piece of good luck—the discovery of Beer's diary—it could not be much amended today. In the matter of the diary Beer is virtually unique among German authors of the seventeenth century, as very few chronicles of this sort have survived. The manuscript, written in his own hand, was found in 1963 in the Erfurt city archives and was sent to Adolf Schmiedecke, then director of archives in Weissenfels, where Beer had spent the last twenty years of his life. Much of the following account of Beer's life is drawn from the diary, which was published in a not entirely scientific edition in 1965.[2]

Johann Beer (also spelled Bähr, Bär, Peer), was born on 28 February
1655, in the tiny village of St. Georgen in Upper Austria, in a charming
landscape of lakes and picturesque mountains, still a favored vacation
region for campers and hikers. It is a gently hilly land, sparsely popu-
lated by European standards, and of an uncommon beauty that Beer
never forgot. The quaint nature descriptions in his works usually depict
not the area around Weissenfels but his old homeland. His father,
Wolfgang, was an innkeeper, and a plaque commemorates the building
in which Beer was born.[3] He was the seventh of fifteen children, most of
whom died in infancy or early childhood. It appears from circumstantial
evidence that the Beer family was perennially strapped for funds. An
evidently autobiographical anecdote in the diary relates that young Beer
was sent for a time to live with his aunt. Later, at about the age of five, he
appears to have been cared for by his grandmother and attended school
for a year in nearby Schörfling.

The Attergau region of Upper Austria where Beer was brought up had
been predominantly Protestant since the sixteenth century, but the
ruling families suppressed Protestantism during the first part of the
seventeenth century, with the result that, nominally at least, the populace returned to the Catholic fold. But Protestantism remained the secret
religion of a significant proportion of the inhabitants, as large numbers
of Austrians left for Protestant areas of Germany toward the middle of
the century,[4] and the Beer family ultimately emigrated, too. The diary
hardly touches on confessional matters, however, perhaps because of
Beer's early education in the famous Benedictine monastery at Lambach,
a magnificent Baroque structure in Upper Austria. He attended school
there in 1662 "in order to study music" as we read in the diary, but we
know his musical education had already begun in St. Georgen. His
education in a Catholic school is explained by Johann Mattheson, an
eminent musicologist of the early eighteenth century and in a sense
Beer's first biographer. Writing with some bias, he reports: "But
because his father Wolfgang, and the mother, Susanna, were rich in
nothing but children, some Papist gentlemen gradually attracted the
sons of these parents with a view to converting them to Roman beliefs."[5]

Beer remained at Cloister Lambach for three years, but he says
disappointingly little about this formative time, providing in the diary
only a list of some of his teachers and schoolmates. In 1665, he went
from Lambach to Cloister Reichersperg am Inn, where he continued the
study of music, and in 1669 he went for a year to study at the Latin
school in Passau at the expense of a friend of the family. In the meantime,
his parents had taken a fateful step for their son, who otherwise would

probably have gravitated to the court in Vienna: they emigrated, probably in 1668 or 1669, to the then predominantly Protestant city of Regensburg, in southern Germany. In 1670, the fifteen-year-old boy, now trained in the fundamentals of Latin and music, joined them in the vibrant, colorful city where he was to remain for six years.

The Regensburg period was extremely important for Beer, because he was suddenly plunged into a remarkably variegated cultural life in a city with scores of churches, nunneries, monasteries, and towerlike, loopholed patrician homes—a quaint and interesting mixture of architectural styles: Romanesque, early and late Gothic, as well as Baroque. The Roman remains had apparently not yet been uncovered. Even today the city presents a romantic appearance, with its many towers, steeples, the narrow bridge across the Danube, the venerable inns and hostelries, and the narrow, winding streets and alleyways. Its street plan, in fact, has changed little since the time of Beer. The Imperial Diet—which met in Regensburg from 1663 until 1806—drew to the city large numbers of ambassadors and their retinues from all over Europe, men with exotic tongues, and, to the Regensburg burghers, exotic dress. It was a place of pomp, ceremony, feasts, parades, entertainments, and music, in short, one of the most stimulating cities in Europe.

Music was a much more important aspect of public life then than now, and the presence of so many Protestant and Catholic religious institutions—with their constant demands for composers and musicians—made the city attractive for the practicing musician, especially for one as well-trained and as talented as Beer, whose musical abilities were likely responsible in part for his admission to the *Gymnasium Poeticum*, a prestigious Protestant school founded in 1538. Its demanding curriculum included Latin, music, mathematics, and philosophy.

From this time on, Beer's life is better documented than in his earlier years. We know that he received room and board in the *Gymnasium* in return for musical services such as singing in the boys' choir. He was also learning to play stringed instruments and had embarked on a modest musical and literary career. There was an active theatrical life in Regensburg, stimulated no doubt by Jesuit drama; and we may assume that Beer's literary appetites were whetted by performances he saw. He reports in his diary that he wrote three "comedies" in Latin while at the school, and that he could write such works at the drop of a hat, although he says that they were of no consequence. He also wrote a number of poems, some set to music, which were commissioned for the funerals of prominent Protestant citizens of Regensburg, a large number of them exiles like him. We also have good reason to believe that he wrote a

German comedy or opera with the title "Mauritius Imperator," which has apparently not survived.

Beer was a precocious, energetic, resourceful, and ambitious young man. He was also something of a cut-up, as recently discovered archival records show. The archives are those of the Regensburg Protestant *Gymnasium*, now in the possession of the Lutheran Church there. They contain the minutes of a meeting concerning school matters dated 2 December 1675, which report in the stiff chancellery style of the time one of Beer's pranks:

After Philipp Jacob Seylin [Seulin], Cantor [. . .] orally made the complaint that the students, contrary to school regulations, left and reentered the school at night without his permission, or that of the school inspector, [. . .] and sometimes stayed out the entire night, [. . .] and upon being reprimanded, [. . .] responded by writing lampoons against him, as had recently Johann Beer, and that the students played tricks on him, for instance by banging on the school door, as if something unusual were going on: [. . .] for which reasons he [Seulin] requested the school superintendent to give the students a stern warning [. . .].[6]

The tricks played on the cantor Seulin may have stemmed from causes less innocent and childish than might be inferred from this document. Beer repeatedly attacked an unnamed cantor in his satirical novels, and there is good reason to believe that he was taking literary revenge on his former instructor because Seulin had appropriated or plagiarized one of Beer's musical compositions.[7] There are other connections between Beer's school life and his writings; thus the figure of the mischievous but essentially good-hearted student recurs in the early novels. But the most important connection is that at the Regensburg *Gymnasium* Beer recognized his talent for amusing his fellow students with humorous and fabulous tales derived from his reading of German chapbooks and his own experiences as an innkeeper's son, traveler, and schoolboy sent from school to school. Life was far from easy for the boys at the school, particularly for those thirty, more or less, who were earning their keep by singing in church, at weddings, funerals, and performances, and by sweeping up, winding the clock, running errands, and the like. They must have found Beer's storytelling a welcome respite from long hours on school benches and at music rehearsals. There is substantial evidence that Beer was a "spellbinder." In the "Dedication" to his friend and fellow pupil Sebastian Mylius,[8] in the novel *Ritter Spiridon* [Knight Spiridon, 1679], he writes:

The wild stories occasionally told for fun in our conclaves I set down on paper and spent most of my time [after leaving Regensburg for Leipzig] with such invention.[9]

On the title page of the novel, which served as advertising in the seventeenth-century book fairs much as the "blurb" on the dustjacket does today, Beer, or his publisher, enumerates the features they hoped would attract his contemporaries: "tournaments, [. . .] murderers' castles, robbers' dens, adventures, discourses on love, tales of hermits, ghosts and such things."

The diary scarcely touches on the last two years of Beer's Regensburg period; we learn merely that he at first intended to attend the university at Altdorf[10] and that he took an oral examination in the magnificent medieval courthouse in Regensburg on the basis of which he was awarded a stipend to study at the university in Leipzig. The record of that examination still exists[11] and shows that the twenty-year-old Beer was questioned chiefly on theology and musical theory, and was called upon to speak extemporaneously on the subject of the errors of the Jesuits. This curious document tells us much and nothing; we see once again that Beer's principal interest and preparation lay in the field of music, and yet we cannot determine how probing his questioners were, or how well qualified they may have been to examine him, or for what purpose he intended to study in Leipzig. And the remark on the Jesuits leads nowhere, since, as was previously mentioned, Beer does not air confessional questions in the diary.

Once in Leipzig, Beer spent only a few months as a student in the university. One can conclude from apparently autobiographical passages in his novels written or conceived in Leipzig that the new student was bored and lonely. And so, rather than devoting himself to his studies, he wrote his comic "inventions." Countless passages in Beer's novels satirize neoscholastic syllogistic methods that had lost their pedagogical value and had become mere exercises in hairsplitting. Students in Beer's novels typically have been addled by their studies, their arguments being absurd, their behavior arrogant or boorish or befuddled, or all three. In short, the academic world does not come off well in Beer's works, probably because its distance from the practical world, its smugness, insularity, and religious-political orthodoxy were an abomination to the imaginative, gifted climber. The university grind was not to his liking; music and writing were his first loves.

Fortunately, his musical talents became known in Leipzig, no doubt through his own efforts. As a result he was offered a position in the court orchestra of Duke August of Saxony-Weissenfels in October 1676.[12] As a talented singer, performer on stringed instruments, and somewhat experienced composer he must have been a welcome acquisition for the orchestra. The fact that his presence in Leipzig coincided with the reorganization of the court orchestra of Saxony-Weissenfels[13] was of supreme importance for his career.

In 1669 the orchestra had consisted of nineteen musicians; it was enlarged at the order of Duke August of Saxony-Weissenfels, probably because he wished to compete with the grandeur and artistic institutions of the court of the Elector of Saxony in Dresden. This was no easy undertaking, for the Dresden orchestra, which had been directed from 1617 until 1672 by no less a figure than Heinrich Schütz, was considered by many to be the most accomplished orchestra in Europe.[14] And since the prestige of the court was closely linked to the quality of its orchestra, the social status of court musicians had risen in the course of the century, in stark contrast to the lower social status of the city musicians, who were generally organized in guilds. Acceptance of a post at court, as opposed to a similar position in the city, had extramusical advantages for Beer that, considering his lifelong class consciousness, must have weighed heavily in his decision.[15] It appears, however, that he was negotiating with the city council of Regensburg after having accepted the ducal position. The council made no offer, however, and became annoyed with Beer because his university studies and his study at the *Gymnasium* had been financed by the city with a view to his returning there. This incident is mentioned specifically more than once in Beer's novels, and he generalizes on the court-city conflict as a topic of broad interest to the rising middle-class or "professional man" of the late seventeenth century in several of the novels, and particularly in his theoretical work, *Musical Discourses*, which appeared nineteen years after his death. In one chapter, entitled "Why heretofore many cities cannot get what they desire in the way of musicians," he describes a young, penniless musician (doubtless himself), whose talent is neglected by the city and who therefore "glides into a princely port."[16] The data concerning Beer's negotiations can be gleaned from letters in the city archives of Regensburg, but his diary mentions only a three-month visit with his parents in 1678.[17]

Little is known of Beer's activities between 1676 and 1678, but external evidence shows that he must have spent a significant part of his time writing "novels,"[18] for in the period 1677 to 1685 he wrote the bulk of his twenty-one works (some in two parts, one in four!) in this genre. In 1677, ten years after the death of the greatest German novelist of the century, Grimmelshausen, there appeared Beer's *Der Symplician-ische Welt-Kucker oder Abentheuerliche Jan Rebhu* [The Simplician World-Observer or Adventurous Jan Rebhu]. As the title suggests—the adjective "Simplician" derives from the title of Grimmelshausen's *Simplicius Simplicissimus* and its continuations—Grimmelshausen's influence dominates the first work as it did most of Beer's subsequent picaresque and adventure novels. *Jan Rebhu* and the other picaresque novels, such as *Corylo*, *Pokazi*, and *Jucundus Jucundissimus*, were paralleled by a series of ironic novels of adventure, patterned somewhat on the immensely popular *Amadís* novels, but constituting, in fact, parodies on the novels of romance. Shortly after Beer joined the court in Weissenfels he turned away from the picaresque genre to a more serious form, that of the "political novel."

One of the few verifiable facts about this period is that Beer was engaged to Rosina Bremer, daughter of the deceased owner of the Black Bear Inn in Halle, on 7 November 1678. On 17 June of the next year they were married. Now Beer was a novelist, composer, musician, owner of an inn, and, as of 22 March 1680, a father. Ten more children followed the first, but, as was so often the case in this period, only six of them survived their father.

The death of the reigning duke of Saxony-Weissenfels on 4 June 1680 brought about important changes in the lives of all those associated with the court, including Beer, since Duke August's son and successor, Johann Adolf I, who was to reign from 1680—97, now actually undertook the long-planned relocation of the court from Halle to the new capital of the Duchy, Weissenfels. That the court should be moved from an important city and cultural center such as Halle to what was little more than a provincial village occurred because while Duke August had jurisdiction over the city of Halle as long as he lived, upon his death it became a part of Brandenburg. August had therefore begun years before his death to develop tiny Weissenfels (population 1663: circa 800)[19] into a proper residence. It would then house still another of the hundreds of courts that existed in the German empire at this time. As early as 1660 the foundation for a new castle, the "New Augustusburg," was laid, and in 1664 a *Gymnasium* was founded. But while steady preparations for a move had long been underway, the actual relocation profoundly changed the nature of the sleepy town. In addition to the extensive building program,[21] the most important components of which were the castle (in effect an office building for state officials as well as a ducal residence), the court chapel, and a *Gymnasium*, there were less obvious, but no less significant, changes. Worldly, experienced, and well-educated men of court came to Weissenfels—one wonders if many of them did not come with great reluctance to this obscure corner of the duchy—and an extensive, carefully ranked and tiered court hierarchy was established.[22] Beer writes of the relocation that a good number of the court musicians at Halle did not follow the court to Weissenfels, but that he, his wife, child, and brother arrived there "in unbelievably cold weather."[23]

Beer was twenty-two at most when he wrote his first novel, and there is every sign that up to the time of his arrival in Weissenfels he had led not an easy but a carefree existence in which student friendships and outrageous pranks played an important role. The lightheartedness of his novels attests to this fact, as does the above-mentioned incident concerning the practical jokes played on Seulin. But once at court, even at this relatively small one, Beer assumed substantial responsibilities and saw life from a different perspective. He made numerous trips with Duke Johann Adolf in the following few years to villages and cities in the surrounding territory; and his diary shows that he was fast becoming a valued and popular man at court, at least in the eyes of the Duke. There are indications in his novels and in polemics written against him that he may have been involved in feuds with persons at court or in the town, but no documentary evidence has thus far come to light. We also learn from the diary that he was expected not merely to perform musical duties but to act on stage, to tell stories, to amuse his table companions, to advise and to act as companion to the Duke and to write occasional poetry. He had already written funeral poems for prominent Regensburg Protestants in his student days, and now he was called upon to write obligatory poems about such events as the erection of a church tower at the ducal palace. It was the price one had to pay. But early successes at court as well as his musical ability resulted in his appointment in 1685 to the post of concertmaster, which meant that he was second in rank only to the conductor, Johann Philipp Krieger (died 1726), a well-known composer in his own right.[24]

But with all his responsibilities, and in spite of the dour religiosity that pervades much of his diary, Beer must have remained a cheerful, even jovial man, since contemporary documents dwell on this aspect of his personality. Erdmann Neumeister, who knew Beer personally, wrote in his Latin survey of German Literature[25] of Beer's predilection for wordplay: "He makes especially elegant jests in the form of puns."[26]

And Beer himself emphasizes his natural high spirits in the polemic *Ursus murmurat* (1697)—drawing attention to the contrast between his outlook and that of the severe rector Vockerodt—thanking God first that he was born in the Christian faith and second that He gave him a cheerful frame of mind.[27] And there are occasional passages in the diary that reveal the playful side of Beer, such as his account of a visit to the Wartburg, Martin Luther's hideaway in Eisenach:

> I wrote in the very room where Luther stayed, and put the following on the wall:
>   Johannes Beer / also came here
>   The fourteenth of September was the date
>   One wrote the year 1688.[28]

On the whole, Beer's diary, as bare and laconic as it is, reveals a very busy, ambitious musician and courtier who seemed to enjoy many aspects of life at court. There is evidence in the later political novels that he was disillusioned by the plotting and sycophancy endemic in courtly circles, but there is also evidence in his novels[29] that Beer either had had bitter disputes with the townsfolk of Weissenfels or that he had bitter recollections from Regensburg, or both. The relationship between the citizens of the little town—which now chiefly functioned to service the court and its ever-increasing bureaucracy—and the individuals who lived in the town, but whose loyalties lay with the court, was not always cordial. There is much in the Weissenfels archives touching on the town council's hostility toward Johann Riemer, Beer's contemporary, a novelist and professor in the ducal *Gymnasium*. For instance, the city council blocked Riemer's construction of a house on a lot purchased by him, on the grounds that the building of a house at that location could adversely affect the town water supply. The actual reason appears to have been the publication of novels by Riemer that portrayed middle-class tradesmen, shopkeepers, and city officials as narrow-minded dolts.[30] Since Beer also wrote novels critical of the humorlessness, corruption, and lack of imagination of the stolid middle class, we can assume that he too was made to feel the displeasure of his fellow citizens. To what extent he participated in civic affairs in Weissenfels we do not know, but the entries in the diary indicate that he found his fulfillment in court life. Certainly there was sufficient activity at court:

> Today you've got to go with the court there, tomorrow to another place, it makes no difference whether it's day or night, and doesn't matter whether it's raining or the sun is shining [. . .]. Today one has to go to the church, tomorrow to [perform at] the banquet table, the day after tomorrow to the theater.[31]

The picture is evidently not exaggerated. The court orchestra had to provide music for church services, for ceremonial dinners, for the opera, and for the theater, where the musicians were also called upon to act.[32] There was considerable travel; trips to Leipzig, Gotha, and Jena are mentioned in the diary. There were quiet periods during times of mourning, but on the whole the last two decades of the seventeenth century were extremely active ones musically at the Weissenfels court. Alewyn determined that between 1679 and 1720 at least seventy-six different operas were performed there. Beer himself wrote the libretto for an opera performed in Coburg, *The Chaste Susanna*, and seems to have composed the intermezzo for one other opera.[33] He certainly had a reputation as a fine musician and composer beyond the boundaries of Saxony-Weissenfels; the diary reveals that other courts attempted to lure him away.[34]

Beer's musical propensities and training played an important role in his literary works: there are dozens of musicians in the novels, and his language is replete with musical metaphors, used even in the most banal situations, such as descriptions of animal sounds, and the like.[35] He also inserted his musical theories and biases into the novels—Beer was perhaps a more talented theoretician than performer or composer—and made veiled and uncomplimentary references to other musicians of the time whose views he did not share.[36] He used the novels to emphasize the social and musical distinctions between well-trained musicians who enjoyed the largesse of court and city on the one hand, and vagrant musicians—Beer would call them charlatans—on the other, who were roaming about Germany in large numbers. Beer intended in his writings to justify, or even glorify, the role of music at court and in church, for he saw the reputation of respectable musicians being tainted by wandering "beer-fiddlers," as he termed them.

He had to fight on two fronts, for toward the end of his life he was unexpectedly confronted with a Pietist attack on music. This came in the form of a polemic written by the Gotha school rector Gottfried Vockerodt (1655–1727) in 1696. As rector of the *Gymnasium illustre*, with its over nine hundred students, among them the sons of some of the most eminent intellectuals of the time, Vockerodt was an influential personality. He expressed his views, which were based on the writings of the polyhistorian Athanasius Kircher (1601–80),[37] in *Missbrauch der freyen Künste* [Abuse of the Fine Arts, 1697]. Both Kircher and Vockerodt were disturbed by the emotional power of music, claiming that Alexander the Great and King Eric of Denmark (Eric XIV, 1533–77) were brought to the point of madness by it. Hence, musicians can have a dangerous influence on the course of nations, Kircher argues. He provides as an example the decline of the Greek city states which coincided with the increasing affective component of music, what today we might call its "Dionysian" aspect. He also cites the decline and fall of the Roman Empire in the reign of Caligula, Claudius, and Nero, who "ruined themselves with such music."[38] The triumph of Christianity brought a reversion to simple, pure music that alone is conducive to virtue and solemnity.[39] The early Church therefore forbade all instrumental compositions and permitted only the most pristine vocal music.

This was the historical background assumed by Vockerodt when he surveyed the profound musical innovations of the seventeenth century, changes which, it goes without saying, he saw as symptoms of decline and decadence. Like Plutarch, Vockerodt argues that the well-trained musician should follow the ancient Greeks and be thoroughly familiar with the principles of philosophy so as to know "which manner of creating music is most proper and useful."[40] Vockerodt says, in effect, that music must retain its ties with the other arts and with ethical principles. "To tear the words of song through superfluous artifice and affected coloraturas" is nothing more than "a vain titillation of the senses."[41] His ascetic views, medieval in effect, had considerable influence among the straitlaced orthodox Lutheran clergy, who would certainly have been in the majority at that time, with the result that he evidently succeeded in discrediting opera and even instrumental church music for a period of years in the province of Thuringia.[42]

Beer, in musical matters a progressive, made light of Vockerodt and his adherents in two prose satires, *Ursus Murmurat* (1697) and *Ursus Vulpinatur* (1697). In these works, as in many of the novels, he derides academic methods of argumentation and reliance on classical and Church "authorities," saying that the theories of the ancients have little relevance in this issue, that the older theories on music cited by Kircher are not supported by empirical data. Beer's debate with Vockerodt is essentially a confrontation between modern empiricism, so far as musical theory is concerned, and the remarkably late survival of medieval scholasticism.[43]

It was mentioned previously that Beer is one of the very few German writers of the period who left behind a record of his life. As terse as it usually is, and in spite of the fact that it reveals nothing about his own novels or about his feelings toward his wife and friends, it is significant in revealing what he considered worth setting down. Unfortunately, there is no detailed description of life at court, no word on Beer's relationships with his publishers, his thoughts on his own writings and

those of his contemporaries, nothing on his literary theory or practice, no
description of street scenes or gatherings in inns or council meetings in
Weissenfels. In fact, Alewyn wrote a short introduction to the Schmiedecke edition of the diary which hardly conceals his disappointment that
the jottings are not more revealing. The entries are often so laconic and
vague that our curiosity is piqued rather than satisfied. For instance,
there are references to court dress and decorum (one follows the "Spanish" model on Holy Days),[44] to an apparently converted Turk, Wilhelm
Schein, who was married at the castle in Weissenfels,[45] and the statement
that "on the 1st of August I went to Halle where I heard the so-called
Pietist [August Hermann] Franke preach and heard the famous philosopher Christian Thomasius debate."[46] Lacking entirely are Beer's *reactions*
to the new customs or dress at court, to the conversion and marriage of
Schein, even to the appearance and rhetorical skill of Thomasius, one of
the great reformers and enlighteners of the century. And for the modern
taste Beer seems to attribute undue significance to the sensational, to
robbery, murder, executions, and the "miraculous." Immediately following the entry on Thomasius, he lists eight cases of accidental death,
murder, and various forms of manslaughter. His own family gets short
shrift, as the diary limits itself to dates of birth, baptism, and death of
his children and relatives, together with customary pious expressions,
such as "God rest his soul."

Just as the brevity of his remarks about his own family reveals
a peculiar mental toughness or insensitivity of the time, Beer's fascination with the tragic aspects of daily life, with the bizarre, the
grisly, the "supernatural," clearly also reflects the *Zeitgeist*, as even
a cursory examination of seventeenth-century German literature will
show. Accounts of inexplicable occurrences and meteorological oddities
were popular reading matter in sixteenth- and seventeenth-century
broadsides; the learned Nuremberg writer Harsdörffer's *Der Grosse
Schauplatz Jämerlicher Mordgeschichte* [sic] [The Great Theater of Ghastly
Tales of Murder, 1650–52], a translation-adaptation of stories from
Romance sources, was one of his most popular works. Even the literary
giants of the century, Andreas Gryphius and Grimmelshausen, had a
pronounced taste for the gruesome: Beer in this regard is a child
of his time but his morbid interests may go somewhat beyond the
norm.

On the 30th of August in Wengelsdorff [not far from Weissenfels] a maid was
executed by sword. She had killed her child while it was still in her body by
means of herbs meant to cause abortion.

On 17 September two brothers beat a peasant from their village to death. The argument started at a dance here.

At an execution, at nine o'clock, an unmarried fellow had his head chopped off for manslaughter. I wasn't too far away when he died. [. . .] whosoever shall spill human blood, his blood shall also be spilled.[47]

However sophisticated the Weissenfels court may have been—at least relative to the superstition and general backwardness of the surrounding provincial villages—and no matter how much Beer had become part of it, he retained until his death an unsophisticated curiosity and even morbid interest in violence and the supernatural that probably derive in part from his upbringing in rural Austria. Although he received a good education in Latin literature in his early youth and in Regensburg, and, judging by autobiographical passages in his novels, was widely read in the literature of the period,[48] he attended the university only for a short time. So that while there is much in his outlook that is sophisticated, and more erudition in his writings than has generally been recognized, he remained a "country boy" in many respects, and his heart remained in rural Upper Austria. In short, while Beer was a man of many talents— in addition to those already enumerated he was, as the sketches in the diary attest, a skillful draughtsman— he can be said to have remained, somehow, unfinished, a "diamond in the rough." This holds not only for the young, but also for the mature Beer. He reports, for instance, several mysterious "foreshadowings" of the death of Duke Johann Adolf in 1697, including a nocturnal din caused by a *Poltergeist*, the appearance and disappearance of a woman in white in the ducal palace, a vision in the court theater, and two ominous dreams in one of which the Turks besieged Weissenfels, while in the other the duchess dreamed of an eclipse of the sun. These dreams are related with almost literary polish, and were not taken lightly by Beer.[49] I do not wish to imply that he was uncommonly superstitious; his observations appear to reflect the outlook of the upper and middle classes in Germany at the time.

The new Duke, Johann Georg, reached his majority in 1698; by all reports his reign was even more extravagant than that of his father. Beer remained the boon companion to the son that he had been to the father and does not comment on his profligacy.[50] Johann Georg, a patron and practitioner of the arts,[51] was also high-spirited and fun-loving, propensities that made Beer a natural confidant. We repeatedly read of gifts made to him by the Duke and of the elaborate and expensive fetes mounted for the latter. An account survives of three weeks of festivities

held in Weissenfels on the occasion of the marriage of the Duke in
January 1698:

On 13 February there was a magnificent banquet, on the 14th an opera was
given. On the 15th there was a comedy and a gala. On the 18th a carnival and
open table. The procession in the carnival [a kind of parade or procession]
consisted of: 1. A Moorish King (Duke Johann Georg himself) with a band of
Moors and Moorish music under a canopy. 2. The Muscovite Tsar (it was Prince
Christian [a brother of the Duke] . . . and music. 3. A band of Romans. 4.
Ancient Germans in old-fashioned clothing. 5. Miners. 6. Hussars. 7. Tatars
[. . .] on the 19th of February there was an animal hunt in the garden and a
comedy. The 20th open table with a masquerade with all sorts of instruments.
[. . .][52]

And so it continues through the third of March! Beer reports similarly
elaborate entertainments in May of the same year, consisting of mind-
numbing doses of theater, opera, and dancing.[53] To what extent these
activities brightened the drab existence of the middle-class artisans and
peasants in and around Weissenfels or contributed to their tax burden, or
both, is difficult to say. There is no sign in the diary that Beer felt these
feasts and comedies to be wasteful or even unusual, but there is evidence
in the novels that he was consciously dealing with problems and injus-
tices brought about by class distinctions and that he was acutely aware of
the conflict between Christian values and the new pragmatism that
informed court morality.

   Perhaps Beer was too grateful to the Duke to be critical. He writes in
the diary that in August 1698 the Duke gave him a silver watch for
arranging a serenade for the Duchess, and that on the same evening, at
3:00 A.M., he went riding with the Duke and they lay down to rest under
a tree in an oat field after the ride. Not many days later the Duke popped
by Beer's home at 5:00 in the morning after a gala of some sort and stayed
there, with his ducal oboists presumably dispensing music the while,
until seven![54]

   In view of these facts, it appears that Beer and the Duke were on the
best of terms, at least in this period. This intimacy and secure position
might account for the fact that it was about then that Beer began to
publish again, writing theoretical works on music, the polemics against
Vockerodt, and possibly the novels that appeared in the year of his death
and posthumously.[55] Beer apparently cut such a good figure at court that
he almost certainly hoped for a patent of nobility as a reward for his
musical accomplishments; Chapter 50 of his posthumous work "Musical
Discourses" bears the title "Whether a Musician Can Be Raised to

the Nobility by Virtue of His Talents?" His answer; "Why not? For whether the sword or the pen makes one noble, who can deny this [ability] to the noble art [of music]?"[56]

The mysterious circumstances surrounding Beer's diary—no one knows how it came to be in the Erfurt archives—and the very survival of the documents are curiosities in themselves, but it is a unique oddity in German Baroque literature that Beer should have set down, on what turned out to be his death-bed, the chain of events that led to his death. During a shooting contest near Weissenfels on 28 July 1700, he writes, the musket of a certain Captain Barth accidentally discharged, the ball striking the organist Heinrich David Garthoff and then him. Beer died on the sixth of August and was buried on the eighth, at the age of forty-five.[57] He was survived by his widow and six children. The funeral was held in Weissenfels and, in accordance with the custom of the time, the funeral sermon was printed together with poems written by his friends and colleagues.[58]

Chapter Two

The Chivalric Parodies: *Hopffen-Sack, Adimantus, Spiridon*

Origins and Influences:
The Chapbooks and the *Amadís*

In obviously autobiographical passages of his novels Beer relates how, on long evenings, he told stories of knighthood, adventure, ruined castles, and ghosts to a close circle of fellow students in Regensburg. The painful separation from these friends when he left for the University of Leipzig may have been the main stimulus for the creation of his first novels: unable to *tell* his stories, Beer wrote them down.[1] Their absurd and comic plots and the slapdash way they were written lend credence to this theory. But, as seemingly frivolous, even puerile, as these earliest works are, they represent a type of novel whose best-known European example, Cervantes's *Don Quixote* (1605; part II, 1615), is widely considered the first great novel: the chivalric parody.

Both Beer's novels and Cervantes's masterpiece are symptomatic of a significant shift, at least among "intellectuals," from credulity to skepticism regarding the historical accuracy of the events reported in novels of knighthood. The works of both authors make light of the still popular chivalric prose romances such as the twenty-four volumes of the *Amadís* cycle (appearing in Germany in 1569—95), and they do so in large part for the same reason: these tales of knighthood have little relationship to actual medieval chivalric values; they are anachronistic, escapist literature, laced with eroticism and magic—the latter more offensive to German clergymen of the time than the former—and offensive to adherents of the Protestant work ethic because they are addictive, hence not only morally pernicious but, worse still, a waste of time.[2] We know from passages in his novels that Beer was an avid reader of the *Amadís* and of German chapbooks (largely of Romance origin) such as *Fortunatus*, *Melusina*, *Emperor Octavian*, and *Till Eulenspiegel*. The term often applied

16

to these prose tales, chapbook (*Volksbuch*), is so broad as to be meaningless. The most serious shortcoming of both the German and English term is that it does not distinguish between the dignified style of chivalric "chapbooks," the "romances," and the earthy, folksy tone of the humorous, "pre-picaresque" books. But the word *Volksbuch*, being an invention of Romanticism, was unknown to Beer, and his attitude toward these works of the fifteenth and sixteenth centuries was more discriminating than that of the Romantics. He found some merit in those "Histories," to use his term, that smacked of historical fact, and scorned those that do not, even though they might claim the authority of historical chronicle.[3] If one can judge from passages in Beer's novels, the implausibility of most chapbooks was that element that at once irritated and amused him most. While he owns to having been an avid reader of the tales in his youth and seems to recall them with nostalgia, in maturer years he viewed them from a different standpoint: as a well-educated and sophisticated man of the world with the practical biases of the Protestant middle class.

It seems to have been a literary vogue of the time among "enlightened" authors to inveigh against the *Amadís* and the chapbooks; that Beer also does so is therefore not surprising, although his remarks can be misleading if one takes them to be a blanket condemnation of the tales that enraptured him as a boy and allowed him a temporary escape from the narrowness and poverty of his life. Some of his statements about the chapbooks are of more than biographical interest since they provide some of the best evidence available that the chapbooks were still a favorite form of entertainment in the second half of the seventeenth century, that the practice of reading aloud to women spinning yarn or to other manual laborers as they worked existed in some localities, and that servants may even have read such books while they performed repetitious tasks.[4] Amusing tales helped to relieve that monotony and melancholy endemic in provincial German life to which Beer so often alludes in his novels. And entertainment, after all, is a legitimate function of literature, as even that most earnest enlightener Weise was to say in his "poetic" of the political novel, the *Kurzer Bericht vom politischen Näscher* [Short Report] of 1680. So that, in short, Beer's feelings about the chapbooks were ambivalent: he harbored fond memories of hours lost in their pages as a boy, but as a well-educated practical man he is likely to have felt that to resist enlightened views would amount to obscurantism. His ambivalence is not a crucial point, for the main target of his parody was not the chapbook, or even the relatively sophisticated *Amadís*, but another literary phenomenon, as we shall see.

While *Hopffen-Sack*, *Adimantus*, and *Spiridon* parody the improbable action, heroic exaggerations, and idealized motivation and characterization of the *Amadís*, its imitators, and certain of the chapbooks,[5] they also poke fun at stylistic aberrations that were not characteristic of the chapbooks of knighthood. The chapbooks therefore cannot be the sole, or indeed primary object of Beer's satires. This confusing situation can best be explained by examining the work that best exemplifies Beer's literary parody or travesty, his *Printz Adimantus*.[6]

Smitten with love for the incomparable—an accurate term, as we shall see—Princess Ormizella,[7] the gallant Adimantus, the "knight of Love" as he is called, for such titles are *de rigueur* in the *Amadís* cycle, arrives in Spolta to joust in a tournament. He hammers the armor of his opponents with such vigor that "the nearby powder magazine had to be watered down to prevent damage from this frightful combat."[8] After Adimantus has proven his mettle in combat, there is a magnificent banquet; during the subsequent dance Ormizella, no Victorian wallflower, opens her heart and boudoir to our hero:

"Because you love me [as I do you], take this proof of my favor, which is that you shall appear tonight in this room once it is dark. Here on the right are my chambers; it is there that you will learn who Ormizella is. Be silent, and dance a bit more nimbly, holla!"[9]

As arranged, Adimantus goes to Ormizella's bedroom and, in his eager anticipation, wrenches the door off its hinges. A huge weight that the king secretly has caused to be placed over the door—it is the "visitors" door and is never used by her, Beer explains—falls down according to plan, knocking the suitor senseless. Since he cannot now take part in the tournament, Ormizella disguises herself in his armor and proves by her victories that she is as aggressive and daring on a horse as on the ballroom floor. Having recovered, Adimantus sets out on an obligatory adventure to lay ghosts who just this week "killed sixty-eight persons."

The last third of the short novel is an account of the hero's curious exploits with "ghosts, castles, chapels, and towers," as promised on the title page, until the work ends when he is placed under a spell for a duration of forty years. The conclusion of the novel is found in *Ritter Spiridon*: after almost eight years Spiridon succeeds in freeing Adimantus, who then celebrates a magnificent wedding with the patient Ormizella.

The values of the old chivalric books are here turned upside down. Ormizella is a Teutonic Amazon rather than a model of femininity, and

Adimantus, with all his heroism, frequently looks more than faintly ridiculous, as when he rips the door off its hinges. The names of the other knights, "The Knight of the Clover Leaf," "The Knight of the Apple," "The Knight of the Blue Jerkin-Sleeves"; exaggerations of the intensity of combat; and repeated, rote assurances of the veracity of obviously incredible events are some of the elements characteristic of this humorous parody of the *Amadís* and older chivalric chapbooks. *Adimantus* is a significant document in the history of German literature as the earliest travesty of this sort.

The existence of a seventeenth-century German parody of chivalric literature necessarily raises the question of whether Beer could have been influenced by *Don Quixote*. A partial translation of that novel had appeared in 1648, and Beer could have known it, at least indirectly, through short stories of Georg Phillipp Harsdörffer (1607–58) that treat episodes from the Spanish novel. It is conceivable that he used the complete French or Dutch versions. [10] He mentions *Don Quixote* in one of his polemics against Vockerodt, [11] and further evidence of an influence is found in an episode in *Ritter Spiridon* involving an attack on a windmill which Alewyn calls a "crude Don Quixotiade." [12]

Because the action of the novel parodies that of its chivalric prototype it was assumed that Beer's mockery of stilted language was directed at the same genre, that is, at the *Amadís* and its relatives. These writings had already been under fire for some time from academics and clerics who condemned their "immorality." Their popularity, or social acceptability, had declined among the upper classes since the beginning of the century. [13] And in *Adimantus* Beer too speaks of the "poisonous Amadis," but he may have been speaking ironically or, if not, he was referring to the content, not to the style, of that work. As was noted earlier, the preciosity attacked by Beer is not typical of the chivalric chapbook, nor is this style found with any frequency in the *Amadís*. [14] There are some clues to the real object of Beer's parody in passages within the novel.

Some of these appear in the first sentence of the preface, where the author uses metaphors involving genitive constructions whose humor lies chiefly in the discrepancy between the stilted construction, so typical of the affectations of courtly and chancellery style, and the banality of its actual meaning. Beer tells the reader that if he offends him in manner of description or style "you may take the dung of my coarseness on the wheelbarrow of your benevolence to the water of forgetfulness [. . .]." [15] Metaphors of this kind are used throughout *Adimantus* to parody techniques recommended by seventeenth-century poetics and used in the flowery rhetoric of court. [16] Another modish device, parodied even more frequently by Beer, is that of the composite noun used as a poetic circumlocution. In many instances these compound nouns are more or less absurd neologisms of Beer's own invention; we find in *Adimantus*, for example, *Stall-Karpffen* ("stall carp") for "horse," *Wasserkürisirer* ("water cuirassier") for "crab," and the more conventional *Sonnen-Vasal* ("vassal of the sun") for "moon," *Papier-Pflug* ("paper plow") for "pen," *Wort-Farb* ("word paint") for "ink," and *Tageleuchter* ("day chandelier") for "window," the last term being a much-ridiculed invention of the novelist Philipp von Zesen (1619–89) to replace the customary word *Fenster*, which he correctly identified as a loan word. Zesen's proposal for linguistic "purification" came to naught because of the inertia of tradition and because he failed to realize the extent of the debt owed by German to other languages.

Beer's parodistic use of these composites, an important aspect of his earlier novels, can only be judged in context, as in this passage from *Adimantus*:

So bald nun Morpheus vom Abend-Essen aufgestanden und mit dem rechten Arm in den Sternen-Rock gefahren, erblickt der Ritter auff seiner linken fünff Fingerträger, das ist auff seiner lincken Hand, einen grossen Pulver-Fresser, das ist ein grosses Feuer [. . .]. Je näher sich nun Adimanto dahin begabe, je stärcker fienge sein Stall-Karpffen an zu schnauben, biss er endlich wie ein Wasserkürisirer, das ist wie ein Krebs, zurückgienge. [17]

(As soon now as Morpheus had arisen from dinner and had thrust his arm into his starry cloak, the knight sees on his left five-finger bearer, that is on his left hand, a great powder-eater, that is a great fire [. . .]. The nearer Adimantus came to it, the more violently did his stall-carp rear, until it finally was going backwards like a water-cuirassier, that is, like a crab.)

Passages like these will puzzle the reader unfamiliar with seventeenth-century recipe books for the writing of literature. While these poetics differed somewhat from one another, as a group they left little scope for the individual poetic imagination—probably Beer's strongest suit— urging, rather, imitation of classical (i.e., Latin) models and rhetorical principles of structure, organization (of the parts and the whole), and adornment. This last word touches an aspect of Baroque style that, in literature, amounts to an endeavor to surprise the reader pleasingly by connecting seemingly disparate objects or concepts in striking metaphors—as in English metaphysical poetry—or to express the mundane and prosaic in mannered expressions such as "sun vassal." Stylistic adornment concerns us most because Beer's ridicule of the *stilus ornatus* is a basic motif in his works.

The presence of Zesen's neologism *Tageleuchter* among the composite nouns in *Adimantus* leads to the assumption that Beer's parodies were directed primarily at this novelist; he would not have been the first to ridicule Zesen.[18] And there is evidence in other works of Beer that points in that direction. In his posthumous theoretical work *Musicalische Discurse* (1719) the word *Tageleuchter* is mentioned scoffingly in connection with Zesen as an example of the absurdity of purist linguistic reforms. The reformers, zealots, as Beer saw them, were attempting the impossible task of cleansing German—admittedly a chaotic language in the seventeenth century—of words of foreign origin. In *Jucundus Jucundissimus* too there is a humorous reference to two neologisms of Zesen in the speech of a peasant playing the role of Cupid in an impromptu comedy.[19] The new coinages of Zesen—*Reit-Puffer* ("riding shooter" for "pistol") and *Tageleuchter* again—do not rhyme as they should with other words in the poem. To produce the rhyme one has to substitute the customary German words *Pistole* and *Fenster*. In the same novel Beer replaces the words Jupiter and Venus with *Götter-Printz* ("prince of gods") and *Göttin der Liebe*[20]("goddess of love") where only the "foreign" words yield a rhyme.

Beer probably chose Zesen as a target since he was the most prominent advocate of impracticable linguistic reforms. But the central object of his attack emerges from numerous passages. In *Corylo* he criticizes affectations in style "as, for example, when they should say: when the sun came up, they write: The tender dawn began now to spread its first light of the day, that now was commencing, across our earth [. . .]."[21] In the second part of the same novel he writes in the preface: "I was not so much interested in the ornateness of the words as in the matters themselves." In part four of the *Welt-Kucker* he touches again on this theme: "I have heard too that I do not write as decorously as Barclay,"[22] but this innocuous remark takes on fuller meaning when we compare it with a passage from the *Winternächte*. In this later novel Beer attacks the "history books" and their "affected courtesy [and] stilted word order."[23] Beer then gives as an apparent example of such style Pastor Bucholtz's interminable pious alternative to the *Amadís*, the courtly novel *Herkules und Valiska* (1659). Beer's criticism includes, but is not limited to, the courtly heroic novel, as his satirical treatment of contemporary poetics indicates. In *Welt-Kucker I* a village priest links ornate circumlocutions with earthly vanity—the connection, seen philosophically, is not as remote as one might assume—and with the *Amadís*. [24] He belittles books that claim to teach the art of poetry in a few lessons and gives absurd examples from a fictitious poetic treatise with the title *Der unvergleichliche Poët, das ist: Eine Invention von denen abentheuerlichsten umschreibungen der Wörter* [The Incomparable Poet . . .]. [25] In the *Winternächte* he heaps scorn on poetic rules that would put "forceful restraints on youth" [26] and has the protagonist stumble across such a poet's primer, excerpts from which reveal it to be a travesty of the worst examples of late Baroque poetics. [27] These and other passages in the novels and theoretical works confirm Alewyn's hypothesis that Beer's criticism of the poetics is a criticism of "objective art from the spirit of the subjective experience [of life]." [28] Beer's natural creative instincts bridled at the farfetched metaphors, pompous or precious circumlocutions (such as Zesen's "waterhouse" and Siegmund Birken's "wooden-horse" for "ship"), [29] and similar stylistic oddities to which he must have been exposed as a boy in the Regensburg *Gymnasium*. His opposition to the poetics must date from this period since his criticism of them begins in the earliest novels.

Beer's attitude was no isolated one; in this matter too he owed much to Moscherosch, Grimmelshausen, and to lesser-known figures such as Johann Schupp (1610–61) and Georg Wilhelm Sacer (1635–99). These culturally conservative "Old Germans," as they are called, rejected poetics, elaborate, highly adorned language, and pastoral poetry (and Petrarchistic conventions) primarily because they connected these literary phenomena with French modes and manners, with Machiavellism, and with new artistic trends coming from Italy. A work that might have influenced Beer particularly is Grimmelshausen's *Der teutsche Michel* [The German Michel, 1672], which rejects Zesen's suggested reforms and standardization of the German language and at the same time glorifies virtues such as frankness and honesty that since the time of Tacitus had traditionally been associated with the German national character.

Next to Grimmelshausen the most significant literary influence on Beer was Christian Weise, whose condemnation of excessively ornate style and advocacy of clarity and simplicity had a salutary, wide-ranging effect on German letters and hastened the transition from the heavy, overladen, or overdecorative style typical of the German courtly novel of the late seventeenth century to the relative clarity of the "new style" prescribed by the much-maligned tastemaker Johann Christoph Gottsched (1700–66). One passage in Weise's novel *Die drey ärgsten Ertz-Narren der gantzen Welt* [The Three Worst Fools in the Whole World, 1672] illustrates his kinship with Beer: in an inn, the protagonist happens upon a clutch of love letters written in a saccharine, obsequious style. They parody the then very popular manuals for the writing of "gallant" love letters and make use of the same sort of absurd genitives with which Beer regales the reader in *Adimantus*.[30] And in the very next chapter we find a parody in epistolary form of Zesen's style and orthographic reforms.[31]

A few final words on *Adimantus*, a modest, even immature work more original than of literary merit. In spite of its unusual character—in fact, it is unique in German literature—the novel shows Beer's dependence on major literary figures, and is a significant manifestation of a trend toward simplicity of expression in the late seventeenth century.

Hopffen-Sack and Spiridon

Ritter Hopffen-Sack appeared in the same year as *Adimantus*, and its motifs and themes also come from the chivalric, supernatural world of the *Amadís* cycle. The young hero and narrator, a student in Toulon, comes upon a ruined castle, is exposed to the hocus pocus of ghosts, flaming skulls, magic formulae, and an encounter three hundred miles beneath the earth with an enchanted knight. The latter is awakened from his spell by the hero, who is rewarded with a magic ring that will grant virtually every wish. By means of the ring he whisks himself off to Constantinople and literally tweaks the beards of Turkish sultans, places millstones about the necks of twenty-four rampaging murderers, changes swords into foxtails with comical results, and makes himself invisible in order to overhear the foolish deliberations of a town council on the regulation of the church choir. The motif of invisibility is exploited in this and similar scenes to deal satirically with provincial ignorance and self-importance and with other issues of particular interest to Beer (especially those touching on music), but then Hopffen-Sack rides off again to the make-believe world of knighthood to take part in a tournament. The protagonist's ring loses its power and he must beg for his food; he becomes a servant, wishes he were lying with one of the maids, finds himself in her bed but without the ring (which has inexplicably regained its power), and is condemned to death for sorcery. He awakens to the sound of the school bell on 1 April and finds the entire story was a dream.

Again, this is a light-hearted, imaginative, humorous but trivial work whose origin was likely an evening entertainment for the pupils of the Regensburg *Gymnasium*. The naiveté that characterizes the chivalric episodes of the earliest novel, the *Welt-Kucker*, has in this work already given way to gentle irony. This work differs from *Adimantus* chiefly in its lack of unity: it mixes elements of the picaresque and chivalric genres. In addition, we find sociocritical themes as well as clearly personal allusions.

Ritter Spiridon, the last of Beer's "chivalric novels," provides not only a tale of adventure but also a happy ending to the story of Adimantus. The introduction of pirates and robbers, the use of disguise, the separation and reunion of lovers, mistaken identity, and single combat are the same as those found later in the great German courtly novels, although here they appear in much simplified form and can be said to point forward to the adventure novels of subsequent generations.

Chapter Three
The Picaresque Novels

It is extremely difficult to apply customary definitions of subgenres to the novels of the seventeenth century and especially to the unorthodox novels of Beer, even in those rare cases where there is some agreement on the definitions. Since Beer's chivalric parodies are unique, they alone present no difficulty in this respect. But the discussion of those novels that are labeled "picaresque" raises problems. The most bothersome of these is the difference of opinion among scholars as to the meaning of the term "picaresque." Some use the term broadly, applying it to any novel in which the young protagonist takes a journey in the course of which he has a variety of experiences with individuals from every social stratum. This attractively ahistorical, imprecise definition leads to the categorization as picaresque novels not only of *Lazarillo de Tormes*, *Gil Blas*, and *Roderick Randon*, but also of *Don Quixote*, *Candide*, *All Men Are Brothers* (a Chinese novel of the thirteenth century), *The Pilgrim's Progress*, *Tom Jones*, and *Tortilla Flat*.[1] The narrower, more precise definition derives chiefly from the first Spanish novels of roguery, the anonymous *Lazarillo de Tormes* of 1554 and Mateo Alemán's *Guzman de Alfarache* (Part I, 1599; II, 1604), the latter novel appearing in an immensely influential translation of Aegidius Albertinus (1560–1620) in 1615 that introduced the genre into German literature. The realism—one might say naturalism—of these works is a drastic departure from the aristocratic perspective and idealism of the chivalric and pastoral novels that by and large dominated prose fiction in the Romance countries until around 1600. One may argue that the rise of the modern novel coincided with the emergence of realism, with the description of the brutality, bestiality, and poverty of the peasant world and of other unpleasant social realities, and with the portrayal of unsympathetic but all too human fictional figures who appear for the first time in the picaresque novel. Alexander Parker's definition of the genre is one of the best:

[The pícaro] relates his life-story, generally from his childhood, in the form of an autobiography constituting an episodic narrative rather than a unified one. The autobiographical form, although adopted by the majority of the picaresque novelists, is not essential; the distinguishing feature of the *genre* is the atmosphere of delinquency. This begins in a setting of low life but generally ascends the social scale; the origins of the protagonist are usually disreputable; he is either born or plunged as a youth into an environment of cheating and thieving, and learns to make his way in the world by cheating and thieving in his turn.[2]

The picaro is a rogue and rascal but not a villain. There is little or no character development in the picaro, who typically serves a series of masters, some of whom are just as poor as he is and some at least as roguish. Hunger is a leitmotiv of the picaresque form, often placed in the foreground in exaggerated descriptions of the gauntness or feebleness of the protagonist. The hero or, more accurately, the antihero, is resourceful, cunning, and amoral. Society has made him so through harsh experience as an orphaned or abandoned youth. He may reach relative affluence and be cast down again by fickle fortune. In any case, he has little control over his future. The world in which he lives is fraught with inconstancy and uncertainty. When the picaro comes to this realization he sees the errors of his ways and, in the "classic" models, feels remorse and may attempt to do penance by withdrawing from the company of man. This situation obtains to varying degrees in several novels by Beer: the *Symplicianische Welt-Kucker* [Simplician World-Observer], which appeared in four parts between 1677 and 1679; *Corylo* (two parts, 1679–80), *Pokazi* (two parts, 1679–80), *Jucundus Jucundissimus* (1680), and a work that probably appeared posthumously, *Bruder Blau-Mantel* [Brother Blue-Coat, 1700]. My discussion of these works will, however, not revolve around their generic properties, as it would be a mechanical and fruitless exercise to dilate on how they compare with the earliest picaresque novels or to analyze each element of the work that is more typical of other subgenres, such as the chivalric, pastoral, or political novel. After all, the terms now used to describe types of novels arose only after the definitive works in the genre had come into being. Beer never spoke of writing novels of roguery any more than of writing political novels; the labels arose after the fact. What is more, there are very marked traits of the novel of roguery in a large number of Beer's other works, particularly in several political novels and in the two Willenhag novels. In short, while one cannot ignore the very significant formative influence of the genre, I prefer to let the works speak for themselves, since each has its own peculiar subject matter and structure.

Der Symplicianische Welt-Kucker

Beer's *Symplicianischer Welt-Kucker* appeared in four parts between 1677 and 1679, the entire work having the length of a moderately long novel. There is a great variety of subject matter: allusions to aesthetic and religious concerns of Beer, references to other literary figures, signs of involvement in virtually every cultural or literary issue that would preoccupy him in the remainder of his works. Because of its thematic richness, and because it is his first novel, and one of the best, I will discuss the work at some length.

The Simplician World-Observer—the adjective "Simplician," as mentioned, a reference to Grimmelshausen's masterpiece[3] and probably chosen in the hope of stimulating book sales—is, like *Simplicius Simplicissimus*, partly autobiographical but betrays a variety of literary influences, including the Spanish picaresque novel, the "political" novels of Christian Weise (see Chapter 4), the seminal work *Gesichte Philanders von Sittewalt* {The Visions of Philander von Sittewalt, 1640—43] by Johann Michael Moscherosch (1601—69), and the chapbooks of the fifteenth and sixteenth centuries. Like Grimmelshausen's novel, Beer's work is related in the first person by a narrator presumably telling his story long after the events described occurred. This narrative technique has the advantage of vividness and immediacy, but also the disadvantage of inconsistency, since there are discrepancies as to tone and moral stance between those portions of the narration stemming from the now mature, "converted" picaro and those passages that relate events freshly and with no didactic ballast, as though they had just taken place. While the *Welt-Kucker* is by no means a picaresque novel in its purest form, it and other novels of Beer owe much to that genre in their structure, characterization, narrative technique, and the element of delinquency mentioned so prominently by Parker. From the dedication of the novel one is given to understand that it has a didactic purpose: through the errors of Jan Rebhu, the protagonist, narrator, and fictional author of the work, the reader is to learn the evil paths that he should avoid so as not to endanger his immortal soul. As in the early picaresque novels, one of the main premises of Beer's novel is that temporal goods are of only apparent value, that they are fleeting and inconsequential in the face of what Andreas Gryphius called "eternity, thou word of thunder!" This is the philosophical *donnée* of Albertinus and of Grimmelshausen. Beer mentions another purpose of the novel, one consonant with the poetic theory of Weise, which, in turn, derives from classical and Renaissance poetics: literature should entertain as well as instruct. There is evidence that a significant function of the literature of the late medieval and early modern period was not merely to amuse but actually to dispel melancholy and depression. One encounters this statement of purpose in prefaces to books printed in that period too frequently to dismiss it as the repetition of a calcified formula.

Typical of the time is the introductory metaphor describing the protagionist as a plaything of fate thrown up and down like a ball. It is a truism of the picaresque novel that man's destiny is determined by forces beyond his control. The narrator says that he comes from a well-known family in Upper Austria, which of course corresponds only geographically to the facts of Beer's life. Other details are not autobiographical: Beer's father was not killed in the Thirty Years' War, nor did his mother die in his childhood, as does Rebhu's mother. Here we see the influence of Grimmelshausen's *Simplicissimus*. But decidedly autobiographical is Rebhu's early interest in music, a central concern of this and other novels of Beer.[4]

Somewhat unusual in this novel is the prominent role played by the erotic. Rebhu is involved with several women, a circumstance that leads—repeatedly—to his remorse, contrition, and renunciation of society. Curiously, each of these erotic adventures is connected with his activity as a musician. Music is clearly related to the sensual. Beer appears simply to state this as a fact without further reflection and without laboring the point. One must bear in mind, after all, that he was only twenty-two when the first part of the novel appeared. And since his work was obviously influenced more by Grimmelshausen's *Simplicissimus* than by any other book, it seems likely that the depiction of the erotic in that novel left its mark on the *Welt-Kucker*. Simplicissimus is made to pay dearly for his adventures of the flesh; his youth, initial innocence in sexual matters, and subsequent repentance is precisely reflected in the seduction and love affairs of Jan Rebhu.

The *Welt-Kucker* is a complicated work, partly musician's novel, partly adventure story, partly picaresque novel. As we shall see, it also has elements of the political novel. The hero, early orphaned, is left to the not very tender mercies of relatives. He leaves them, and, through the mediation of an innkeeper, finds a position as servant and pupil to a *castrato*, a musician at a provincial court.[5] The boy accommodates himself to the decadent ways of the court, becoming, as he puts it, "more proud and arrogant" all the time—this is a remark of the mature narrator, one of many brief, moralizing asides that cause the inconsistency of viewpoint mentioned before. A fabulously beautiful Italian countess living not far from the court meets Rebhu, is mightily attracted to him, and sets about to seduce him.

This early section of the novel treating the love affair with the countess is written with considerable skill, especially in the subtle, suggestive way in which Beer reveals, step by step, the calculating, lascivious character of the countess.[6] On one occasion she sends Rebhu a silk shirt with silver buttons and tells him through her servant and confidant, a dwarf, to "keep quiet" about the rendezvous and to come to her lodgings that night. If the reader is not immediately aware of the implications of the invitation and gift, the signal "keep quiet" surely alerts him. But Rebhu is at best subliminally aware that something is amiss. The morally dubious nature of the hero's meeting with the countess is again signaled when we read that the "girl" sent to lead Rebhu through dark streets and alleys to her room is none other than the dwarf. The darkness of the scene, the squalor of the alleyways, the fact that they enter not by the front door, "like honorable persons," but by a side door, all point to the equivocal nature of the assignation. There is even a certain symbolism in the portrayal of the lodgings of the countess.[7]

Descriptive details contribute to the erotically charged atmosphere of the setting, such as the "frivolous paintings of naked men and women" in the lodgings, and the remark of the dwarf after they arrive in the countess's boudoir that the large bed is "an excellent" one. But when the boy meets the countess, it becomes apparent that even her considerable skill as a seductress is insufficient to overcome Rebhu's innately good moral sense. Obscurely aware that she plans something unsavory, he tries to leave. But she gives him a sleeping potion with the result that he finds himself, unclothed, in another bedroom the next morning. He is unaware of what has occurred during the night and therefore is still essentially innocent. He returns to the court, where there is much discussion of contemporary musical issues, with the result that the momentum of incident and plot maintained to this point is lost for a time.

A typical aspect of Beer's later works is already evident in his earliest novel: his lively, exuberant, animated style—which often uses musical terms with humorous effect—a profligate, Rabelaisian heaping of words, a zest that, as one writer pointed out, "would be hard to parallel in German literature between Fischart and the Romantics."[8] There are other aspects of Beer's style and manner that recur in virtually all his later novels: his frequent humorous use of student Latin, a macaronic mixture of German and Latin, comic neologisms, rich use of slang, the pun, dialect, coarse language, and peculiarities of speech, such as the heavily Italian-accented German spoken by the countess. Finally, a considerable portion of the work consists of learned, or quasi-learned, discursive conversations reminiscent of those popularized by the prolific Georg Philipp Harsdörffer in his *Gesprechspiele* (1641−49).

After the party with the musicians, during which scurrilous musical tales are told with much gusto, the aforementioned castrato—himself enamored of the countess [!]—questions Rebhu about her and sees that she has taken a fancy to the unsuspecting boy. When she sends a request a week later, asking that Rebhu come to her lodgings, the castrato warns him against going, saying he will lose not only his voice but also his immortal soul. To get him out of the way, the castrato sends Rebhu to the castle of a nobleman. At such a small court each musician has a menial job to perform in addition to his artistic one, and Rebhu is hired both as a soprano and as a page. He fares very well, rapidly gaining the favor and trust of his master, a jolly nobleman. Oddly enough, the life he leads with this nobleman corresponds in many respects to the occasionally riotous life that Beer himself actually was to lead with the Duke of Saxony-Weissenfels in the 1690s. Rebhu and his master hunt, fish, make outings incognito, or, with the page dressed as the nobleman and vice versa, drop into bustling inns and play pranks on the peasants (for this is the first in a series of Beerian prankster-noblemen); and all the while Rebhu is treated as though he were the nobleman's son.

Elements of the adventure novel occur frequently in this section where we encounter the first of several ghosts, the specter in question assuming the form of a fiery man who haunts a gloomy forest. This and many other archaic or supernatural motifs, such as the joust, the dungeon and torture, the enchanted forest, magical groves, and buried treasure, show the link between Beer's novels and the chapbook and folk tale of the late medieval period, although more often than not these motifs are treated tongue in cheek. This spectacular element will have made his novels more popular, but one should not dismiss the presence of the supernatural as mere commercialism, nor is it always treated ironically.

At the castle, years pass happily, but Rebhu's equilibrium is destroyed by the beautiful noblewoman Squalora—her rather unsavory name a typical device of Beer—and as he succumbs to her charms he indulges in moralizing digressions on the faithlessness of women. We find in Beer's earliest work a conservative, indeed reactionary attitude toward women, an antifeminist attitude in the mainstream of German satirical writing from the late medieval period; yet, in the same work, we find playful— one is tempted to say rococo—touches, such as secret letters written in the new gallant style, courtliness of behavior, and erotic titillation, that anticipate techniques of the gallant novel of a later period. When Squalora asks Rebhu to give her music lessons, the instruction is carried out in a "very Simplician manner," that is, she instructs him in something quite different. It is at this point, rather than in the episode with the Italian countess, that Rebhu ceases to be an innocent, and in accordance with folk beliefs of the time the hero loses his soprano voice. Beer would have us believe that this phenomenon brings the matter into the open. Squalora advises him to leave, giving him money and jewels; he steals away into the night.

Rebhu stops for a time with a village priest, a "thoroughly pious" man, and is exposed to his homilies on contemporary culture. Although it comes to light that even this paragon of virtue committed some youthful indiscretions, his statements contain social and cultural criticism reflecting Beer's own sentiments. It is interesting to see what the young author perceived to be pressing issues of the time.

Anticipating Christian Thomasius's (1655—1728) criticism of the German university system, the priest contends that it is not necessary to attend a university to acquire learning, and he mentions eminent personages, such as Augustine, who had no university education. Attending a university can be harmful; the student may overeat, drink to excess, duel, and fall into the meshes of women. In the common-sense manner of Thomasius, the priest attacks the neoscholastic traditions doubtless hammered into Beer in the Latin schools and in Regensburg and repeatedly parodied in his novels. The preacher considers that man to be the best theologian who is the most pious, not the most learned. As to literature, he opposes the appearance of heathen gods in contemporary poetry. If the preacher is Beer's mouthpiece—and I feel he is—these views reveal in his earliest novel a problem with which we shall have to contend in almost all his works: the marked tensions between liberal-progressive and conservative-traditional viewpoints. In a conservative vein the priest also attacks decorative circumlocutions then fashionable in poetry. The poetics of the seventeenth century emphasize that when one writes of sublime events or persons he should not name an object in a commonplace way but should use his wit and imagination to devise artful metaphors for the word in question. As Harsdörffer writes in his *Poetischer Trichter* [Poetic Funnel, 1650], one could call death the "strangler of men," or the "enemy of life," or "the debt of nature." These are among the simpler turns of speech. Somewhat more ornate are expressions for bee (the "industrious little honey-bird") or for honey ("the sugar juice of the flowers" or "the little bees' golden fruit in waxen parchment"). Overused as it was, this poetic technique quickly becomes tedious. It is this stylistic tendency, euphuism, that Beer strikes out against here and in several of his later novels, as well as in *Printz Adimantus*. The priest's admission that in his youth he dabbled in poetry but found it "nothing but vanity," as it had no higher purpose or redeeming social value, is a significant statement of the young Beer's own view of secular poetry. The priest advises Rebhu to avoid poetry; if he writes at all let it be in the genre of the satire or novel, since these are "not only amusing to write but amusing to read."

This digression is abruptly interrupted by two musketeers who ride up and abduct Rebhu. After traveling for some hours they come to a ruined castle in a "horrible wilderness," a favorite setting in Beer's novels. Imprisoned in a musty tower, Rebhu hears rattling chains and battling knights, and on the next day sees four men being boiled in a kettle. Soon thereafter the Italian countess enters the courtyard with her trusty dwarf, and Rebhu is summoned to a room hung in black cloth. The dwarf accuses Rebhu of having revealed the affair with the countess not only to the castrato but to the entire court, an indiscretion that will now cost him his head. Rebhu begs for his life—he is only eighteen, he says—and says he had revealed the liaison only to Vitali, the castrato. His tears seem to move the countess, but in the meantime Beer provides an explicit account of preparations for the execution, a description that reflects Beer's fascination with the subject but also serves to provide gruesome titillation for the reader. Just as the executioner is about to strike, the dwarf intervenes and Rebhu is led away. He later learns that Vitali had sent the countess an insulting letter with Rebhu's forged signature, hoping through this subterfuge to remove his rival. The countess, who now craves forgiveness from him, promises to make amends by taking him with her to Italy.

They arrive in Italy the very next day, but Rebhu longs for Squalora. At this point he is conscious of the sinfulness of his ways: the observation that "it would have been better for me if I had been beheaded rather than taking up such a life of vice through which I plunged my poor soul into great harm" is that of young Rebhu, not that of the mature penitent. But it is not just his carnal pleasures that disturb him, it is the confused state of his affections. He is madly in love with the countess and also with Squalora. The description of his state of mind cannot be called a subtle psychological analysis, but it is a credible portrayal of a tortured emotional state. Beer's description of Rebhu's struggle with his conscience points forward to figures in two later novels, the *Winternächte* and *Sommertäge*.

Having arrived in Venice, Rebhu, the countess, and the dwarf— throughout a leering, obscene figure and one of Beer's most memorable creations—join the social swirl, attend the theater, and enjoy Venetian nightlife. The hero's former piety is further eroded in the decadent, pleasure-seeking society of Venice—a city of peculiar significance for the

German artist—and, as he puts it, he avoids churches as if they were hospitals. One of the conflicts is temporarily resolved when the countess marries a young, handsome prince from N****. They and their retinue board a ship for the voyage home and are subjected to a storm at sea. Beer, a child of his time, had a liking for symbolism and allegory: just as the hero's earlier imprisonment among ghosts was shown to be a symbolic picture of hell, the sea is compared with "our tiresome life." But the storm abates, and the ship's party lands.

Six month after the marriage, the prince must leave his wife for several days. She invites both Procelli, a Venetian singer, and Rebhu to her chambers, who are discovered there by the unexpectedly returned prince, who orders them executed. But with the assistance of the countess they escape. Rebhu writes Squalora, telling her the entire sordid story, and she answers, saying she awaits him with open arms.

The remaining three parts of the *Welt-Kucker* recount Rebhu's continuing adventures. He attends a university for a short time (as did Beer when this novel was being written), which gives Beer the opportunity to describe student mores. This section of Part II is a stylistic tour de force describing with great energy and heaping of words the stormy life of students. Rebhu continues to regress in a moral sense: while at the university he is merely something of a picaro, but his passion for Squalora drives him to murder. At her insistence, he shoots a man he takes for her husband. The fact that—in a Baroque twist of fortune—Rebhu actually kills a robber wearing the husband's clothing does not alter the fact that he was prepared to take human life. Contrition follows sin like night and day; in the manner of Simplicissimus, Rebhu bids farewell to the world and becomes a hermit. But the desire to return to an active life proves too much for the hero. He becomes tutor to Orbato, a young nobleman, and the two journey to Italy, where Orbato is to pursue his studies, but where in fact he pursues local beauties and has to be extricated from a dangerous predicament by Rebhu. Back in Germany, the hero is to marry Orbato's sister, but she overeats at the marriage feast and dies! After this unglamorous demise it is impossible to take seriously Rebhu's Baroque lament: "I am a ship driven by the immense sea through a thousand unhappy winds because my anchor of hope lies at the bottom." There is another "Adieu, World," this one a bit more convincing than the first, as it contains demonstrably autobiographical allusions, and Rebhu passes a year on a desert island, is captured by Turks, and is rescued by a Christian knight who turns out to be Orbato, now an Amadís *redivivus*. Orbato's taste for foreign fruits this time proves fatal: caught in the bedroom of an Asian princess, he is put to death, but only after Beer has filled several pages with explicit descriptions of the preparations for the execution.

Having escaped, been recaptured, and lived again on a desert island—the repetitiousness of the long novel's chief motifs is one of its signal characteristics—Rehbu, no longer young, becomes the heir of Orbato's mother, and upon her death a wealthy man. Various loose ends are tied up; for instance, Squalora has died after leading a reformed and exemplary life as a respected abbess. Rebhu marries a young girl, and at this point the "manuscript" breaks off; the remainder of the novel is written by his "secretary," who tells us that after Rebhu's marriage he lived twelve happy years until he died eating a partridge (in German, a *Rebhuhn* [!]). He was no ascetic man, we are told, and enjoyed a good joke to the end of his days, but he was a basically good and religious person.

The *Welt-Kucker* treats *in nuce* virtually all the motifs, themes, and issues that occupied Beer in his twenty other novels: carnal pleasure followed swiftly by remorse and the "Adieu, World," knightly adventure, picaresque wandering and change of vocation, haunted castles and gloomy hermit's huts or desert islands, wedding celebrations, the role of music, conversations in lively inns, attacks by robbers and pirates, the penurious protagonist who rises in society, as if in Freudian wish-fulfillment, frivolity and licentiousness of women, the vanity of the world, the pedantry of the neoscholastic university, the obtuseness of provincial and city officials which Beer had observed in Regensburg, the corruption or asininity of some clergymen, the decline of German customs and dress under the onslaught of foreign influences, and so on. Beer seems not to have been interested in working out a realistic, consistent "masterplan" for the novel; in fact, he flaunts his disdain for verisimilitude when he kills off Rebhu's first bride by having her overindulge in food and drink at her wedding banquet and eliminates the protagonist himself in identical manner. The arbitrariness of both occurrences show that the author is playing with his figures. Beer wishes to inform the reader—in rather unsubtle fashion—that the action of the novel is unimportant, that one must seek the point of the work in its satirical and didactic passages.

The Other Picaresque Novels

The other picaresque novels of Beer, *Corylo* I and II, *Pokazi* I and II, *Jucundus Jucundissimus*, and *Bruder Blau-Mantel*, have plots almost as complicated as that of the *Welt-Kucker*, and cannot be summarized here. Like the earliest novel by Beer, they portray young, impoverished, inexperienced protagonists who have to make their way in a corrupt society, but none of them, save perhaps Blaumantel, sinks to the moral level of Rebhu at his lowest point. Like Rebhu, these adolescent heroes bear traits of Beer's own personality but also owe much to literary models. Recurring motifs in these novels include the assumption of the eremitic life out of remorse for past misdeeds, the discovery that the hero is (or is not) of noble birth, and imprisonment in a haunted castle. The novel *Pokazi*, which satirizes the pettiness and absurdity of a city government (Regensburg?), differs from the other novels in its imaginative use of fantasy. A delegation of pots and roasting spits appears at city hall to beg relief from their increasing burden; next to appear are long, honorific titles which likewise complain of abuse and overuse. Beer uses fairy-tale motifs with abandon, having Pokazi sail in an airship at fantastic speeds to fetch a glass of water from the Black Sea. The latter portions of the work depart completely from the realistic norms of the picaresque novel.

Bruder Blau-Mantel is a satirical novel, too, but it stands in the realistic tradition of the picaresque novel. Despite some stylistic tours de force, it is a slight work, one of the weakest of Beer's novels.

Jucundus Jucundissimus, on the other hand, is one of the most readable and carefully planned novels. What is most extraordinary about the work is the power of several passages treating the poverty of Jucundus and the travails of an unnamed student. The following passage calls to mind not only the Spanish picaresque novel but scenes from Dickens:

The roof had holes in it all over, so I had the wind in my face day and night. When it rained I was soaked through and through. I had a small pistol and had a student sell it for me. With that money I had some sausages brought up and ate them immediately, I was so ravenous, together with some beer [. . .]. From time to time cats in heat got into my room, and they carried on their game all over the place. They jumped across my bed, and because I was so weak that I could hardly move, they scratched my mouth and nose badly. When I had to answer the call of nature I had to do it on a roof tile and throw that down on the street. [. . .] After this illness I couldn't do any hard work for two weeks and was spared from fetching beer, chopping wood, and sweeping, and because I still was too weak to go to school I had to stay at home and cull barley, peel apples, unwind yarn, rock the children and so forth.[9]

In this and similar passages, one feels that Beer is drawing upon actual recollections and providing rare glimpses into aspects of seventeenth-century life that are not set down in the disappointingly unrevealing pages of his diary.

The social criticism of the picaresque novels is much more obtrusive than is the case in the Spanish models. The objects of Beer's satire are familiar: pedantry, corruption of the clergy, and the worst symptoms of Romance influences on German dress and custom. None of the works betrays deep religiosity; in fact, the prevailing tone is one of mocking, jaded skepticism toward organized religion. Like Rebhu, Blaumantel and his friend and mentor Pamphilius become hermits at the end of the novel, but Blaumantel's conversion from robber to penitent is too abrupt to be convincing. He may be bidding farewell to the world but not to its comforts, since the two "hermits" will live in cozy quarters, their food and supplies brought to them at regular intervals, paid for with Blaumantel's ill-gotten gains. Symptomatic of the novel's lack of genuine religious fervor is a funeral sermon delivered by Pamphilius which combines pessimism with humor. While it provides a dreary enough picture of earthly existence, Pamphilius has playfully composed it using only words of one syllable:

Der, so hier vor uns tod ligt, ist ein Mann, mit Nahm: Hanss Tropff, die Stadt, wo er auf die Welt kam, ist Thorn in Poln, er war acht mal acht Jahr alt. [. . .] Drum bin ich hier, dass ich euch Danck sag vor die Ehr, die ihr ihm vors letzt thut. Lebt wohl. [10] (He who lies dead in front of us is a man with the name Hans Tropff. The town where he was born is Thorn in Poland, he was eight times eight years old. That is why I am here, to thank you for the last honor you do him. Fare well.)

Chapter Four
The Political Novels

It was mentioned earlier that the term "political novel" is more a critical convenience than the label for an easily definable genre. There are a number of usable definitions, but their drawback is that in delimiting the concept they also have the effect of excluding novels that in some respects are model examples of the genre, requiring the critic, in turn, to explain the inevitable "exceptions" to the rule. Here I use the expression "political novel" in the broadest sense,[1] which includes not only novels with a political message but also those chiefly of a satirical nature. This usage is of course arbitrary and perforce results in a not altogether satisfactory grouping, since the works it links are rather heterogeneous. As to form and structure, these are excellent examples of the "mixed" genres typical of German prose of the late seventeenth and early to mid-eighteenth centuries. Hence, one finds the most disparate ingredients: motifs, figures, and techniques from the chapbook, the "vision" literature, the picaresque novel, courtly and adventure novel, as well as from political literature. I include ten novels in this section, most, if not all of which were completed at the same stage of Beer's development,[2] that is, soon after his arrival at the court in Weissenfels when courtly life and the influence of Weise and Riemer made themselves felt. Their common thread is the element of social satire. Some of the works demonstrate that Beer had at least vague programmatic intentions for the improvement of society along the lines suggested by Weise. The novels include *Der Narrenspital* [Hospice of Fools, 1681], *Der verliebte Europäer* [The Enamored European, 1682], *Der politische Bratenwender* [The Political Turn-Spit, 1682], *Andere Ausfertigung neugefangener politischer Maul-Affen* [The Second Treatise on Newly Caught Political Fools, 1683], *Der deutsche Kleider-Affe* [The German Who Apes French Modes, 1685], and *Der verkehrte Staats-Mann* [The Deceptive Statesman, 1699 or 1700]. A subgroup is made up of strongly satirical works, in which the prevailing tone is that of shrill antifeminism. These are the *Weiber-Hächel* [The Excoriation of Women, 1680], *Jungfer-Hobel* [The Maidens' Plane, 1681], *Bestia Civitatis* [Beast of the City, 1681], and *Der politische Feuermäuer-Kehrer* [The Political Chimney-Sweep, 1682].

We must regard the novels of Christian Weise (1642—1708) as the starting point for the German political novel, regardless of the many ambiguities relating to the nature of this genre.[3] While it is true that the word *politisch*, meaning, roughly, "worldly" and "prudent," even "calculating," was used in German book titles long before Weise wrote his novels, it appears to have been his works, and especially his theoretical work on the political novel, that brought forth numerous imitations. Weise, a brilliant student, then secretary to a nobleman, eventually professor of poetry and eloquence in Weissenfels, redoubtable *Gymnasialrektor* in Zittau, playwright, literary theoretician, and novelist, was one of the most influential men of the epoch.[4] Three of his four novels, but in particular *Die drey ärgsten Ertz-Narren in der gantzen Welt* [The Three Worst Fools in the Whole World, 1672] and his *Kurzer Bericht vom politischen Näscher* [Short Report on the Political Climber, 1680]—the latter work in effect a treatise describing how the aspiring novelist should write a "political" novel—elicited dozens of novels in the last two decades of the seventeenth century.[5]

The works by Weise provide the basis for the definition of the genre, but the ideas that were central to the action of the political novel and that in fact determined the action were not original. The erudite Weise was naturally conversant with the works of Machiavelli, Castiglione, Gracián, Quevedo, Boccalini, and Bacon, to mention only the most significant figures outside Germany,[6] while his native literary tradition provided rich materials in Sebastian's Brant's *Das Narrenschiff* [The Ship of Fools, 1494], with its long catalog of fools (*Narrenrevue*), and Johann Michael Moscherosch's *Gesichte Philanders von Sittewald* [The Visions of Philander von Sittewald, 1646].

The new intellectual currents that Weise mirrored in novelistic form betrayed an increasingly secular outlook, particularly in educational theories, the rise of empiricism and rationalism, which stipulates that, within certain limits, man has complete freedom of will and can determine his destiny. On this point, Bacon naturally comes to mind, and indeed his name is invoked in several prefaces to political novels.

In Zedler's famous *Universal-Lexikon*,[7] a *Politicus* is defined as that man who "is skillful in applying the qualities that serve to gain immediate rewards, such as honor, wealth, and high station, and who knows how to further his own happiness and that of others in a legitimate way." This political train of thought, emanating chiefly from Gracián, Quevedo, and Bacon, found its most significant German popularizer in Weise. In numerous rhetorical treatises and theoretical works, as well as in his novels, he propounded political theories that had application for the bourgeoisie as well as for the aristocracy. He saw the need for an educational process that would prepare the courtier or office-holder for service to the state and came to regard the traditional curriculum of the Latin school, consisting chiefly in the study of the ancient classical languages, rhetoric, and theology, as antiquated. His "practical" view of education confirmed by experience when, leaving the university, he took service as secretary to the Count of Leiningen, and saw at first hand that the demands of public life required training in "gallant," that is, courteous and gracious, behavior, in oratorical ability in German, and the knowledge of geography, law, and French rather than Latin. His educational guide, *Der kluge Hofmeister* [The Wise Tutor, conceived in 1675], which reflects his new perceptions, came about as a result of his activities as tutor to two young noblemen, and it was at about this time that his novels began to take shape, although they were published several years later.

Named professor at the recently founded (1664) *Gymnasium* in Weissenfels in 1670, a prestigious position with professorial rights and court protection, Weise was in his proper element. The Weissenfels school had been founded for the specific purpose of preparing young noblemen and students from the upper middle class for governmental positions. The curriculum was already "progressive" in Weise's sense, and he doubtless began to exercise considerable influence on educational thought, particularly in Saxony, from 1670 until 1678. In this period his political novels appeared, which, together with the *Kurzer Bericht*, were to have an unprecedented effect on the entire novelistic output of the time. He was also in daily contact with Johannes Riemer, who came to Weissenfels as professor of logic and metaphysics in 1673, and who was to become the most skilled writer of the political novel.[8] Weise left two years before Beer arrived in Weissenfels, but his reputation as a scholar and educator (not as a novelist, since he wrote under a pseudonym), as well as the link provided by Riemer, must have made a deep impression on Beer, who had his own thoughts about educational abuses, as will become apparent when we examine his political novels.

Weise's original accomplishment was to transmit knowledge of political life gained through wide reading and personal experience into the Weissenfels and Zittau *Gymnasia* and, through his rhetorical treatises, which for two decades became standard texts in schools in much of Germany, to transmit his theories to a broad public. He was not concerned merely with creating a trained elite for the state bureaucracy but with the application of political rules of conduct in all professions that served the weal of the state,[9] including those of the soldier, the clergyman, the merchant, and even the student. In this context he speaks of gaining one's *Privat-Glück* ("personal happiness") through political means: the calculating methods used by statesmen to anticipate future events and to avert misfortune from the state; the polished demeanor and prudent behavior of the diplomat is to be emulated by the wise burgher.

In Weise's novels, the action usually involves a journey in the course of which the protagonist, an inexperienced youth, is confronted with the inequities, wonders, and harsh realities of the world; the protagonist is usually an observer rather than a participant. He sees, with his mentor, a variety of human personalities, a process that in some novels consists in little more than the presentation of a late medieval "catalog" of fools. The traveling companions then discuss what they have seen, seeking to distill from experience the usefulness of prudence, moderation, practicality, and wisdom in everyday life. These figures are at pains to distance themselves from lower-middle-class and peasant figures, the latter indeed often providing examples of foolish behavior.

Other writings of the period either share Weise's concern with new educational principles as they pertain to the middle-class, as is the case with Riemer, Johann Kuhnau, and Johann Christian Ettner, [10] or they are called political novels simply because they bear at least superficial resemblance to Weise's novels. In my view there is one fundamental characteristic common to all genuine political novels: their didactic intent. Indeed, it may be correct to say that Weise's *Drey Ertznarren* is the "first German novel with the clear intention of enlightenment." [11] This does not mean that enlightenment or education must overtly include discussions of political life, or that it must include the typical grand tour, but that the novels have a concern for the reader's material or spiritual welfare—this is often reflected in the author's tendency to address him directly with the intimate *du* ("thou") form—for otherwise it would not carry out the program spelled out by Weise in his *Bericht*.

Thus far, we have regarded the *Politicus,* the worldly man, only from a positive standpoint. But since the publication of Machiavelli's *The Prince* in 1513 writers attacked the ruthlessness and hypocrisy they felt to be implicit in his *Realpolitik*. The amorality of the state soon attached itself also to the popular conception of the clever courtier who will stop at nothing to achieve his ends. Fundamentalist distrust of calculating, amoral value systems moved writers to publish cautionary, "negative" political novels. [13] In the negative works, traits such as prudence, caution, and moderation play no role; guile, self-aggrandizement, and ambition determine the character of the protagonist. This is one reason why any treatment of the political novel is difficult; the literary term actually applies to two apparently contradictory concepts, one bourgeois and enlightened, and Christian in an ethical sense; the other an over-simplified view of the political man as social cutthroat, the courtier as viewed by the morally outraged conservative. Indeed, these diametri-cally opposed views of man and world lead us to question the frequent characterization of the political novel as a subgenre of the picaresque, particularly in view of the fact that the two forms go their own ways: the picaresque novel or offspring thereof flourishing to the present, and the political novel surviving, in the opinion of some critics,[14] in the form of the most typically German of all genres, the *Bildungsroman*—inade-quately translated as "novel of education"—whose best example is Goethe's *Wilhelm Meisters Lehrjahre* [Wilhelm Master's Apprenticeship, 1795 f].

Among the political novels of Beer can be reckoned three of his weakest works, virulently antifeminist tracts[15] whose stern humorless-ness contrasts starkly with the earlier imaginative novels of picaresque adventure and knighthood. The very titles of these works reveal their harsh antifeminism: *Des berühmten Spaniers Francisci Sambelle wolausge-polirte Weiber-Hächel* (1680), *Der neu ausgefertigte Jungfer-Hobel* (1681), and *Bestia Civitatis* (1681). I include a fourth, longer work, *Der politische Feuermäuer-Kehrer* (1682), even though it concerns itself with broader issues than concupiscence.

As thematically limited as these works appear to us, they seem to have been quite popular when they were published: the *Weiber-Hächel* and *Feu-ermäuer-Kehrer* went through three editions. The subjects they touched must have interested the largely male, middle-class audience: social and sexual issues of the age that cannot be gleaned from historical accounts. Yet the clues which the novels provide about moral tone, tastes, and sex-ual behavior must be interpreted with care, because they are perceptions from the male, orthodox point of view. There was, moreover, a long tradi-tion of antifeminist satire before Beer. There are strongly antifeminist traits both in late medieval literature and in works of the Counter-Ref-ormation. These tendencies are found in works and translations of Aegi-dius Albertinus, an important bridge between the two centuries, and can be followed to Moscherosch, Grimmelshausen, and even Weise.[16] The same vices attacked by Beer were subjected to the satire in that tradition, which also made use of anti-Petrarchan imagery and was frequently coarse and brutal. Beer was most likely using literary models, and his own work was subject to generic conventions that were considerably more binding on the writer of the seventeenth century than is now imaginable.

But this would not account for what appears to be an abrupt decision to write almost exclusively antifeminist satires. While there are traits of misogyny in his earliest novels as well as in his most mature works, he did not devote himself as grimly and dully to the excoriation of womankind as he did in the three works mentioned above. I am inclined to see private circumstances as the motivation for these writings, which came out just after the recently married Beer went to Weissenfels, but one can only speculate as to what role Beer's private life may have played in his writings. Other possible motivations include the author's marked hostility to the stilted love conventions of the "high" courtly novel, so humorously parodied in the chivalric novels.[17] Commercial considerations might also have played a role, a factor that has to be kept in mind when one analyzes most of the literary productions of this period. There was apparently a market for antifeminist works, and one must weigh the possibility that Beer or his publisher felt the novels would be in demand.

In actuality, these works read more as though they had been produced on commission than as a result of Beer's own creative urges. With the exception of a few humorous passages, they are all highly derivative and concentrate on the vice of lustfulness. Borrowed from the political novel is the figure of the mentor.

The plot of the *Weiber-Hächel* illustrates these points. The narrator and author, "Sambelle," comes to a city as a beggar and is taken in by the wife of a goldsmith. The latter is on his death-bed, but his wife, feigning grief, is carrying on an affair with a secretary. Nebulo, the goldsmith's apprentice, plays the role of mentor, explaining the real situation to the unsuspecting Sambelle. As is customary in the political novel, the hero learns through his more experienced friend and teacher how to distinguish between illusion and reality. The goldsmith dies; the hero is horrified and enraged by the deceit and arrogance of women, for hardly a year passes before the widow remarries. After only four months she delivers a child. The marriage ends miserably, and the novel concludes with a warning to the (male) reader to avoid "bad" marriages but harlotry even more.

Bestia Civitatis follows similar structural principles, and is set in the once rich Assyrian city of Nineveh. This work too finds a naive young tailor setting out in the world to find adventure. He has come to Nineveh—sketchily described, as in portrayals of the Holy Land in medieval German paintings, as though it were a German city—attracted by its ancient reputation for depravity. In this modish place he has no difficulty obtaining a position in the shop of a tailor; and he also finds his mentor, a dwarf, who supplies him with abundant scandalous information about the inhabitants. The city is truly a topsy-turvy world, the dwarf explains, where virtue is considered vice, and deceit and nefarious political practices are the norm.

In *Bestia Civitatis* the epitome of concupiscence is a Babylonian whore, the "beast of the city," who is also the wife of a respected citizen. There is nothing exotic about her; in language and demeanor she is very likely modeled on the figure of Corinne in Johann Schupp's *Corinna, Die Erbare und scheinheilige Hure* [Corinna, the Honorable and Hypocritical Whore, 1660], the tale of a woman who raises her daughter to be a whore (Nineveh = Hamburg). "Bestia's" daughter has followed in her mother's footsteps, and both come to the same bad end: they become pregnant and commit suicide. The young apprentice leaves Nineveh on the fourth day of his stay; he has learned important moral lessons.

The fact that *Der neu ausgefertigte Junger-Hobel*[18] is the second work written under the pseudonym "Sambelle" is an indication that crude satires of this sort must have enjoyed some measure of popularity. The first, the *Weiber-Hächel*, had criticized married women; the second inveighs against the loose morals of those as yet unwed. Beer's figures include a nobleman who is bedding down cozily with his cook, but not much is made of this peccadillo, for Beer's target is, again, women. They carry on affairs not only in the nobleman's castle but in town; no social class is spared. And it is the town, not court society, which is the scene of what can only be described as a kind of group sexual orgy.[19]

On the surface, these novels are ascetic, fundamentalist tracts that make use of the novel form in order to find a broader public. Their stated intention is to demonstrate the folly of hedonism and sexual promiscuity so that they may be certain of "an eternal crown of glory."[20] But could there be some other, hidden motive in this and the other antifeminist works? Manfred Kremer sees the antieroticism as Beer's defensive reaction to faint emancipatory stirrings in late seventeenth-century German society. The early Enlightenment was underway, and the percentage of women who had learned to read was increasing[21]—although the absolute percentage was doubtless quite low—and they were evidently assuming an increasingly important role, although still a quite modest one, in public life. In Kremer's view, traditionalist males felt challenged and threatened by this new class of women, and probably were outraged at their "presumptuousness." In this respect Beer too was obviously a conservative. He apparently felt that the best—and only—place for women is in the kitchen and church. There are two scenes in the *Jungfer-Hobel* which bear out Kremer's theory.[22] One occurs when two maids argue about the relative merits of Catholicism and Lutheranism, a

A Capuchin monk and two cousins of Lorenz visit him hoping to make him see the error of his ways , but he scandalizes them by refusing to be examined in the catechism (e.g., instead of answering the question "Who art thou?" with the prescribed "I am a poor sinner," Lorenz answers blasphemously, "I am a nobleman"). He asks what is wrong with listening to old chronicles such as that of Fortunatus: "Ein solcher Ritter will ich noch werden. Danach will ich auf die Turnier zu König und Kaiser ziehn [. . .]"³¹ ("I want to become such a knight. Afterwards I'll ride to the tournament and join King and Emperor"). This illusory world is shattered when one of the cousins, on riding away, fires a blank shot from his pistol. Lorenz falls to the floor in a state of shock, believing himself wounded, and this just after he has boasted: "Cartaunen, Mörsern und Granaten achte ich ohnedem wie Katzengeheule [. . .]!³² ("I pay no more attention to cannon, mortars, and shells than to the howling of cats").

Toward the end of the novel, the narrator tells Lorenz he is going to his ruin. Lorenz agrees and decides to seek stability in marriage. Being rich, he has no difficulty finding a wife. But on the wedding day he becomes as drunk and flatulent as ever; it is clear that marriage will not solve his problems. In fact, very soon thereafter his wife has made a cuckold of him and even makes sexual overtures to the narrator.

The figure of Lorenz fulfills an admonitory function. His neglect of his estate, of his duties as a nobleman, the familiarity he allows between himself and his servants, his impiety, his life of slothfulness: all reveal him to be irresponsible, a social parasite. His shortcomings are all the more conspicuous when compared with Beer's novels of 1682 and 1683, the *Winternächte* and *Sommertäge*, where we find noblemen who do an exemplary job of estate management and by so doing benefit their servants and retainers. Beer makes, in fact, a particular point of this aspect of the nobleman's social role. The characterization of Lorenz as a negative example follows Weise's theory of the political novel set forth in the *Bericht*. Perhaps this reverse characterization accounts in part for Beer's puzzling figure.³³

As unsympathetically as he is portrayed, Lorenz can be seen as a champion of individual freedom, of protest against convention and orthodoxy. It is significant that the alleged crime for which the boy-narrator is so cruelly punished by a sadistic schoolmaster is that same bodily function honed to a state of perfection by Lorenz. While the schoolmaster represents the most repressive sort of outlook, one that was not rare in Beer's day, Lorenz is a free spirit of sorts, his repulsive habit being the ultimate expression of disdain for society. Hence we are bound to view him in a somewhat positive light. In fact, even as the narrator sets down the story, he admits that "ich wünsche mir noch oft in dem Zustand zu leben, in welchem ich damals gelebt [. . .]"[34] ("Even now I often wish I could live the way I did then [. . .]").

If Beer's depiction of the schoolmaster is based on personal experiences, as seems very likely, then the figure of Lorenz must be seen as a fictional projection of the resentment and alienation young Beer had felt. After all, he wrote the *Narrenspital* when he was only twenty-five, and recollections of his adolescence would still have been quite fresh. Lorenz is the embodiment of the eccentric, the independent, unattached hedonist who combines the most disparate qualities. Lorenz is rich but dresses like a beggar; he is cynical but tolerant, incredibly lazy yet on occasion possessed of immense reserves of nervous energy; he is a prankster but also lectures the narrator on social evils; he dreams of becoming a knight and serving king and emperor but is cowardly and scarcely ever ventures out of his castle. The ambiguities of his characterization touched on here are not resolved in the novel. One suspects that Beer himself was not quite sure what to do with this figure, with the result that the novel's message is left unclear.

In the dedication to *Der verliebte Europäer*—aimed at the "world-renowned ladies of Leipzig—the author says he could have entitled the book "Der politische Liebhaber" [The Political Lover], but the title he settled on shows that he also wished to capitalize on the undoubted attraction of gallant love. The title page, again serving promotional purposes, speaks of "Alexander's love-story and brave deeds through which he not only made himself popular with women but also learned the most significant rules of political conduct by means of a tour through various kingdoms in Europe." The book is written "for all curious women [i.e., those having inquisitive minds] and wise courtiers," in other words, for the upper middle class, and particularly for the upward-bound bourgeoisie at court, for whom political *savoir faire* was the key to advancement. The work's depiction of gallant behavior, dress, and speech, which brings it quite close to the later gallant novel, stresses another aspect of "political" behavior. In the "Enamored European" the style is slightly elevated and the action is seen from the artistocrats' vantage point. The protagonist, Alexander, is no chimney-sweep or schoolboy, but the son of the viceroy of Sicily who specifically refers to himself as a *Politicus*.

Alexander, handsome, brave, and intelligent, is sent to learn statesmanship at the Spanish court, then the model of aristocratic etiquette. His first mentor on the voyage from Messina is a Jesuit who explains

why the power of Spain is waning. There are adventures on the way to
Madrid, including that standard ingredient, the battle at sea. In Madrid,
Alexander falls in love with the beautiful Amenia; shortly thereafter they
receive her father's permission to marry. But Amenia dies of grief when
Alexander is forced to accompany the King of Spain on a journey.

The protagonist goes next to Paris and is warmly received at the
French court. Discussions ensue concerning the Dutch wars, about a
ruler's motivation for commencing a war (one reason being, according to
a royal councilor, to rid Paris of criminal elements!), and about the need
to maintain a proper balance of power in neighboring countries. Alexander falls in love with Lukretie, the daughter of a parliamentary
councilor, asks for her hand, and is challenged to a duel by her former
suitor, Comilly. The latter loses and abducts Lukretie, taking her to his
estate near Strasbourg, closely pursued by Alexander—although in the
course of his pursuit the latter takes time to attend a leisurely banquet.
When Alexander learns that, rather than submit to Comilly, Lukretie
has poisoned herself, he kills Comilly in a second duel.

Alexander observes village life in the Strasbourg region, which allows
Beer to satirize the naiveté and pettiness of the schoolmaster, preacher,
and local gentry. We find ourselves now in the small-town atmosphere
of the antifeminist works, where the rustics bear comic names such as
Peter Knackwurst and Hans Fuchs. At a banquet, the protagonist carries
on a political discussion, revealing his religious views, which are critical
of the Catholic Church on three points: that it worships images and
saints, that the laity may not partake of wine at Communion, and that
the laity may not have direct access to the Holy Scripture. On later
occasions, Alexander, a preacher, and several predominantly middle-
class figures carry on table-talk about *Poltergeister*, the devil, and the
nature of women.

Alexander next travels to Vienna. There is conversation at an inn
about the low social status of students, and the nature of university
study, including travel, as a means to education. The next day Alexander
and a companion set out to tour Vienna, but Beer provides scarcely any
description of the city. Instead, there is more learned discussion of
proper education for the middle class and nobility, of the pestilence and
its causes, cannibalism in Brazil and complications for those ingested by
the cannibals once the Day of Judgment arrives. Later Alexander is invited
to the residence of an imperial minister ("I will name him Apulius," writes
Beer), with the result that he falls in love with the latter's daughter. As
Apulius promises to introduce the young Sicilian to the court, the novel
breaks off with the promise of a sequel. No such sequel appeared.

Contrary to claims made in the "Afterword" to the work, Beer provides little in the way of "instruction for the traveler" and even less concerning the "mode of government" and the practices of the courts which Alexander visits. But the novel is replete with discussions of various topics of interest to the reader of the seventeenth century, and is told from the standpoint of the upper classes. These characteristics set off the *Verliebte Europäer* from Beer's previous novels, placing it squarely in the tradition of Weise's novels. Stylistically one finds a dichotomy: the upper classes speak with a certain elegance befitting their station, and since the servants and members of the lower middle class are used for comic effect, as in Baroque drama, their speeches are related in the appropriate lower style. The higher style goes hand in hand with the moral conventions of the idealized hero in the courtly novel, whose constancy is one of his dominant characteristics; he might have come from the pages of a courtly novel.[35] In one important respect his characterization differs from that of protagonists in the Weise novels: he is a man of action rather than an observer. Evidently the chief intention of this novel was the depiction of an exemplary figure whose intelligence, bravery, and political knowledge—Beer distinguishes here between the ethical and unethical *Politicus*[36]—combine the male virtues portrayed in the chivalric chapbooks with those depicted in the political novel. To a lesser extent Beer also provides models of feminine behavior; the anti-feminism of his earlier works surface only occasionally.

Die Andere Ausfertigung, which Beer may not have written, is a political novel in Weise's sense, and a continuation of Johann Riemer's *Der politische Maul-Affen* (1679).[37] It clearly alludes to the misdeeds of actual persons—this is stated on the title page—but is also written according to the well-established scheme of the political journey. In other words, the author is not merely describing things and persons as he experiences them but is shaping scene and action in accordance with the didactic intent of his satire. The novel is much more carefully planned than most of Beer's attested works in this genre.

The first half of *Der dentsche Kleider-Affe* is clearly picaresque. It is unusual among Beer's works, as it is clearly a collaboration.[38] The hero is the narrator; he begins his tale virtually *ab ovo* (from the age of eight months!). His parents are poor peasants who are forced to place him in the none too tender hands of a tailor so that he experiences constant and extreme hunger. There are comically exaggerated descriptions—of his patched clothing, for instance—strikingly reminiscent of the Spanish picaresque novel. The action is simple and episodic; most of the characters are peasants, artisans, or persons who move on the lower fringes of the middle class. The realistic, often crude language of the novel is appropriate to its characters and situations. But the hero is an industrious, intelligent lad who becomes a clerk to the royal treasurer and eventually heir to his riches. The work would seem to be a picaresque novel with a happy ending.

But the *Kleider-Affe* is not primarily a picaresque novel. Beer says in the preface that his intention was to ridicule the "German lust" for expensive clothing and imitation of foreign vogues, particularly those coming from France. The issue of clothing may seem to us a limited, indeed trivial subject for a work of literature, but two facts must be borne in mind: first, that Beer connects the topic of dress *"á la mode"* with a variety of abuses and vices: with flattery, conceit, and exaggeratedly polite or "gallant" conduct at court or in the city, as well as with the excessive use of foreign loan words. In addition Beer's satire relates to specific historical developments. Fashions in clothing, which had changed relatively slowly in the preceding centuries, changed much more rapidly in the seventeenth, the vogue being established first by one country, then by another. The fashion-setting nation in the sixteenth century was Spain, but from the mid-seventeenth on fashions were established chiefly in Paris. Aristocrats naturally set the tone, and the middle class followed their lead within the limitations of their resources and of clothing regulations. The poor did not have to worry about the increasing tempo of sartorial change, as the new fabrics, styles, and accessories, such as perfumed gloves, lace, ornate buttons, and wigs (which evidently became fashionable after 1633 when Louis XIII was forced to wear one after an illness left him bald), were prohibitively expensive.[39] Perhaps the most typical fashion phenomenon of the second half of the seventeenth century was the wig, often imported from France, which became larger and more imposing—that, at least, was the intent—toward the end of the century. The ostentatiousness of the new styles offended Protestant sensibilities, and it is in part this austere spirit which informs Beer's attacks.

There were other reasons, not the least of which was simple patriotism. France had recently invaded the German Rhineland, a fact alluded to angrily in several works of Beer, who probably would have agreed with Defoe, who wrote: "Tis better [. . .] that we should all drink turnip wine [. . .] than that we should drink the best wine in Europe and go back to France for it."[40] Quite aside from the issue of conflict with France, the purchase of foreign goods was a drain on the resources of the country. The hunger of the young hero early in his career stands out all the more because of the luxury of the clothing he must sew and repair.

There was also a conviction among conservative thinkers that effeminate French fashions were being foisted upon a culturally subjugated people. A monk preaches against the subversion of clothing: "That is precisely the cunning maxim of a potentate, that he first teaches the people he wishes to bring under his yoke his language, fashions in clothing and customs [. . .] so that gradually his new rule may seem more tolerable and better than their own."[41]

Der politische Bratenwender is a satirical work combining elements of the traditional catalog of fools, the picaresque, and political novels. Throughout, the protagonist, Schmutzküttel ("Dirty Apron"), remains a poor, abused, mischievous, and constantly hungry rogue. He associates with various other typical picaresque figures: cooks, vagabonds, pages, and tailors. The educational pretensions of the political novel are fulfilled only to the extent that a page and a cook act for a time in the role of mentor to Schmutzküttel and enlighten him about the deceitfulness of the world. Like the *Verkehrte Staats-Mann*, this novel is a court satire of sorts. It gingerly criticizes court life and can hardly have offended any of the courtiers in Weissenfels, especially since Beer uses examples from the Bible and Byzantine history to illustrate his points. About the only imaginative aspect of the novel is Beer's use of an allegorical device, a panoply of "political" kitchen utensils, including the kettle of disgrace, into which, as the cook explains, servants great and small are thrown on short notice; the spit of mercy, which roasts even tough and tasteless meats so flavorfully that everyone wishes to eat from it; the spit of court service, which is used to thrust others from the court and by those who seek positions in government or other favors. This is a nice touch, and the book has other bright spots—some humorous passages that display the author's penchant for wordplay—but Beer did not succeed in integrating his ideas with event and characterization.

Beer's other court satire, *Der verkehrte Staats-Mann*, was published in the year of his death. It shows the influence of the novel of state, the *Staatsroman,* and discusses, in a very broad way, various principles of statecraft. But most of all it shows the influence of Grimmelshausen's *Continuation* (1668) or Book VI of *Simplicissimus*, one of the earliest "Robinsonades." The narrator, a clergyman, has lived as a hermit for six years on the island of St. Helena. His peace is shattered by the arrival of Portuguese settlers, who, ruled by a princess, build a fort and palace. He remains in hiding until he feels morally obliged to reveal himself in order to help a young Portuguese injured in an accident. This same young man, apparently addled by the injury, subsequently emerges as a haughty, cunning, "Machiavellian" upstart who uses all means of trickery including that Baroque staple, the disguise, to clear his path to power. In so doing, he ruthlessly neutralizes the power and influence of a poet, a wise chancellor, and the hermit, placing his pawns in key governmental positions. He poses to the princess as a poet and scholar, is named chancellor, and almost succeeds in marrying her when his chicanery and low social origin—his father butchers swine—is discovered. He returns to Lisbon in disgrace. There he gets his further comeuppance from those he had forced into exile when they swindle him out of a sizeable inheritance.

Another government, the titular head of which is a young, well-meaning regent, comes to power. But actually, the power is in the hands of a governmental secretary through whose person Beer obviously aims to satirize impractical, utopian, "trendy" modes of governance, again revealing his essentially conservative outlook. This first secretary decrees that thieves will not be hanged but beaten to death with goose-wings (coddling of criminals); to prevent adultery no one but the king may marry. Another secretary arrives from Portugal to replace this visionary, but he is a spendthrift, glutton, and war-monger who is fortunately put out of the way by a cannon shot which also awakens the narrator—the action up to this point was all a dream! The ship, which he had dreamt was filled with Portuguese settlers, is actually a Dutch trading vessel, and from this point on, which is around three-quarters through the novel, the hermit discusses his vision with a learned Dutchman. The narrative of the hermit breaks off, and the manuscript is placed in the hands of a publisher by the Dutchman (just as in Grimmelshausen's *Continuation*).

This novel is quite different from the largely middle-class tableaux of the novels of Weise, Riemer, and Kuhnau[42] since it involves no journey, although it has elements of the "Robinsonade," treats the government of the state directly, and, most importantly, portrays the conflict between the *vita contemplativa* and the *vita activa*.

Since this is one of Beer's last novels—although no one can say when it was written—and since the puzzling hermit figure recurs in his novels with such regularity, this last point may be the most important one. In the earlier novels, particularly in the *Winternächte* and *Sommertäge*, several figures are alternatively attracted to and repelled by the life of the hermit. Their bad consciences impel them to an ascetic life, but by nature they are gregarious and feel the tug of companionship, the hearth, and good food and drink. Beer touches on a favorite theme: the question of whether it is man's weakness or his innate desire to be a useful part of society that draws him away from the hairshirt. At the very outset, the narrator cannot help but come out of hiding to help the injured secretary. Beer does not comment further on the event, but his failure to do so, together with the hermit's later involuntary involvement in political affairs on the island, would seem to belie the idea that he can escape the world entirely: "[. . .] and although I considered it no great good fortune again to be a part of human society, it was the emotion of mercy that drove me out of my cave [. . .]."[43] And later, when he cannot avoid becoming involved in the struggle against the Machiavellian secretary, he feels the problematic nature of an existence outside society and comes to the conclusion that "[. . .] he who wishes to be a true hermit must flee not so much men as their vices."[44]

The *Verkehrte Staats-Mann* is laden with didacticism, but offers some notable flashes of humor. One is the characterization of the deceptive statesman, a curious, recurring Beerian type: the nervous, eccentric, cunning, yet subtly unhinged villain whose shifty energy and gift for a spurious sort of eloquence make him stand out from all the other figures. At times one has the odd sensation of having run across a character who has escaped the pages of E. T. A. Hoffmann. This swindler-villain figure[45] is one of Beer's choicest creations and may represent an actual social type endemic in the mobile German court bureaucracy of the late seventeenth century.

Finally, aside from some passages containing stylistic parodies of stiff German chancellery style, there is one episode whose wit and whimsy must be mentioned. It has to do with the second secretary who comes to the island, that fantast who has thieves beaten with goose feathers. Beer's description of this figure and of the dozens of other secretaries under his supervision is a departure from the "realism" usually attributed to the political novel. It is, as a flight of fancy, analogous to the humorous allegorical illustrations used in Beer's *Bellum Musicum* [The Musical War, 1701]. A sample will suffice: "his [the secretary's] cloak consisted of parchment. His pants of blotting paper."[46] His stockings are dyed with ink and instead of a sword he wears quill pens. He is followed by his testy minions, an "alphabet" of secretaries, each carrying a flag on a long pen-holder and armed with ink. If they are "looked at discourteously"[47] they pour the ink in the offender's face "so that a cruelly wide and ugly postscript hung over their nose."[48]

Having seen the weaknesses of many of these novels, particularly those attacking women, one may ask why Beer took the trouble to write them. He clearly was more in his element when writing in the picaresque genre. In part, he may have been motivated by a desire to capitalize on new literary fashions, such as the political novel. But I suspect a more basic reason: Beer's fascination with the efficacy of political tactics and strategies. Beer himself was perforce a political man. Like Riemer, he had risen from humble circumstances to a respected position, not only because of his talent and industry, but because he was obviously familiar with "political" practices and made good use of them. Judging from his writings, however, when political methods came into conflict with Beer's traditional Christian values, the latter prevailed. There is a bluff directness in some of his most sympathetic figures, such as Ludwig in the *Winternächte*, and in his polemics against the pietist Vockerodt that seems incompatible with the circumspect, always-prudent, and, in the last analysis, deceitful behavior of the political man.

Chapter Five
Der verliebte Oesterreicher
and the "Willenhag" Novels

Before concluding our survey with a discussion of the two works that are generally considered Beer's most mature, ambitious, and appealing novels, *Zendorii à Zendoriis Teutsche Winternächte* [Zendorio's German Winter Nights, 1682] and *Die kurtzweiligen Sommer-Täge* [Amusing Days of Summer, 1683], let us first turn to the posthumous novel *Der verliebte Oesterreicher* [The Enamored Austrian, 1704]. This novel resists generic classification, but its numerous thematic links with the *Winternächte* and *Sommer-Täge* suggest a certain affinity with them. In the *Oesterreicher*[1] we find nothing of the chivalric parody, the fantastic or supernatural episodes of the earliest works, nor are there more than hints of picaresque themes and techniques. The novel's chief ingredient is adventure; its hero and narrator, Sylvius, is a participant in all the action, now as warrior, now as gallant suitor. Beer also uses him as his mouthpiece for social criticism—the targets are the usual ones: pedantry, vanity, lust—so that one figure dominates the book to a much greater extent than in any of the other novels. Sylvius also unifies the plot of a work that is about as diversified and involved as can be imagined in a volume of relatively modest length (248 pages).

The salient points of the complex plot are these: the hero, a youth of uncertain origin (he was found as a child of four in a boat floating in one of the lakes of Upper Austria), is adopted by a kind noblewoman who sees to it that he receives a good education. He falls in love with the beautiful, intelligent, and virtuous Countess of Sorona once it comes to light that he too is of noble birth. He wins his bride to be (the novel ends with their marriage) only after outwitting and finally defeating in battle the villain of the piece, Pardophir, who had taken a fancy to the countess. The action of the work lasts over a year, a great portion of that time having being spent by Sylvius as a hermit when he thought the countess dead.

Even this sketchy summary reveals the influence of courtly literature. Indeed, Pardophir reminds one distinctly of the infamous villain Chaumigrem in Anselm von Ziegler's *Die asiatische Banise* [Asiatic Banise, 1689], a gory, titillating work that remained popular long into the eighteenth century. Since Beer's work could have been written as late as 1699, the possibility of a direct influence on Beer from the major German courtly novels cannot be excluded. The *Verliebte Oesterreicher* may show also the influence of the "gallant" novel, frivolously erotic and sensational works, the rococo variant of the grand Baroque courtly novel. August Bohse (1661–1730) wrote fourteen of them, the first appearing in 1685. Since he was employed as a secretary at the Weissenfels court in 1691, there must have been personal contact between him and Beer. These facts, taken together with the sustained elevated style of the *Oesterreicher*—in this regard unique among Beer's novels[2]—and the central role of a love affair, are sufficient grounds for assuming that this novel was influenced by the emerging gallant novel. The hero can make a compliment or turn an elegant phrase as decorously as any nobleman, very much in contrast to most of Beer's other protagonists. Yet Beer changes style abruptly when he moves from love and adventure to satire. The effect is unsettling, not only because one has been transported from the drawing room to the scullery, but because the hero, Sylvius, makes use of both styles according to the social demands of the setting and his function in the novel at that point, and does so instantly and effortlessly. At first one may have the impression that Beer was unaware of these stylistic inconsistencies, but one begins to feel that he intended to play a note or two out of key, to show how false and precious the finely fashioned speeches are, and how they lack the expressiveness of unadorned, earthy German, as when Sylvius says: "Immersed in such thoughts I sat down in a chair and was laden down with as many pangs and twitches of love as a donkey with mill-sacks."[3] For him, this is an uncharacteristically colloquial manner of speaking, and yet it would be typical of such characters as Jucundus or Jan Rebhu, which at once shows how distant the *Oesterreicher* (and to a lesser extent, the *Europäer*) is from the earlier novels and how thin is the layer of gentility in these later novels.

Other requisite types of the courtly novel also appear, strangely transformed, in Beer's novel. Thus, the villain, Pardophir, has been made a bourgeois; his sins are not only those of a ruthless cutthroat or brigand but include those of a middle-class merchant, farmer, artisan, or bureaucrat. The middle-class reader may feel pangs of remorse when the Count of Sorona says of Pardophir: "He knows more about discussing a good pipe of tobacco than prudent ways of running a farm. He only goes to church from habit, and if he doesn't have to go, you'll never see him at mass."[4]

There are elements of symbolism and allegory in all of Beer's novels, but the author seems to wish particularly to draw our attention to them in the *Verliebte Oesterreicher*. The most obvious symbolism is that of the sea voyage, which is expressly equated with the uncertainty of human existence, the tossings and heavings of fate. The first scene of the novel depicts a violent storm on the lake which almost results in the death of the hero. In subsequent chapters there are episodes set on and around the lake; and finally, we learn by a process of delayed revelation that the hero had been found as an infant by fishermen as he floated to shore in a small boat. Elsewhere, the author expressly speaks of robbers in a forest as "living symbols of all children of this earth who lust after pleasure,"[5] and at the end of the work, Beer states *expressis verbis* that the entire work is a symbolic portrayal of human life: "Day and night I lay in great perturbation, my conscience had no peace, my worship no fervor, my heart throbbed in constant sorrow. But what is all this other than a representation of the entire human life?"[6] I previously alluded to Beer's tendency to use certain settings, such as the forest, the castle, the dungeon, and the lake or sea symbolically, the setting in each situation reflecting the mental or moral condition of the hero. The symbolism appears consistently from one novel to the next; its use was no doubt deliberate.

An interesting theme recurring in Beer's novels is that of class barriers. Sylvius apparently has no prospect of marrying above his class[7]—a fact deplored by the author, who repeatedly expresses the view that blood alone does not bestow nobility, using, on one occasion an arch-establishment figure, the Count of Sorona, as his mouthpiece. Describing Pardophir, the count says: "Eating, drinking, and sleeping are his best exercises, which he's studied his entire life, and the opinion that blood alone brings nobility led him to all these vices."[8] The opinion that nobility is based not on an accident of birth but on virtue and intelligence crops up elsewhere, most prominently in a statement of the countess. In praising the musical talent—a quality not mentioned previously in connection with Sylvius and never again touched upon—of a mysterious figure (Sylvius) whom she loves and admires, she distinguishes between nobility of birth and heart: "Sir, few of the nobility have studied this art, [music], for you know well that only virtue can make one noble. So I speak of him not as a nobleman but praise him as a virtuous person [. . .]."[9] To be sure, one can also see in this distinction the basis for a traditional society ruled by the nobility (of blood), but loyally served and presumably spiritually ennobled by the noble of spirit. The countess's coyness prevents a more exact interpretation.

That a personal element is present in these allusions to artificial class distinctions is obvious. One can only surmise as to whether the remarks may have been responsible for the fact that the *Verliebte Oesterreicher* only appeared four years after its author's death.

The "Willenhag" Novels

The *Winternächte* and *Sommer-Täge*,[10] called the "Willenhag" novels after the protagonist and narrator of the *Sommer-Täge*, must be considered Beer's most ambitious works by virtue of their length (over eight hundred pages each) and complexity (over two hundred figures are mentioned). The novels were written at a time when the author, although only twenty-seven or twenty-eight—not so tender an age in the seventeenth century—had learned as much about the craft of writing as he was ever to learn. One must, therefore, consider these works with particular attention when coming to a final assessment of his literary rank. For it is here, critics agree, that he was at his best: most imaginative, self-confident, exuberant, expansive, and concerned with philosophical issues.

I will consider the two novels as a single work, for there can be no doubt that the *Sommer-Täge* is a sequel to the *Winternächte*, in spite of the fact that the names of the characters are not identical and that the works appeared under different pseudonyms. The *Sommer-Täge* picks up the strand of action just where it had been left at the end of the *Winternächte*, although Beer provides the second novel with a brief introduction that lists the "new" figures—most are those of the *Winternächte* with altered names—and sets the scene for the sequel in a manner independent of the first novel. The narrator of the novels, Zendorio in the *Winternächte* and Wolffgang von Willenhag in the *Sommer-Täge*, remains the central and unifying figure in both works. His wife, Caspia, appears in the second novel as Sophia. A Falstaffian figure named Ludwig in *Winternächte* is renamed Philipp in the sequel. A pious Irishman of the earlier work appears in the *Sommer-Täge* as an ascetic Scot, Friderich; and Zendorio's closest friend, Isidoro, as Gottfried.[11]

That Beer thought of the *Sommer-Täge* as a sequel to the earlier work is proven by the otherwise inexplicable fact that in several passages of the *Sommer-Täge* figures are referred to by the names they bore in the *Winternächte*.[12] We do not know at what point the idea of a sequel arose, but it is possible that the commercial success of the *Winternächte* caused Beer or his publisher to think of a sequel. This explanation is not totally satisfactory, however. The *Winternächte* went through only one printing, probably of one thousand to fifteen hundred copies, not matching the popularity of several other novels by Beer, so that it does not appear to have been a signal commercial success. But financial considerations may have figured in the decision to leave the conclusion of *Winternächte* "open," and they may have influenced the final form of the sequel as well. If the second novel were clearly a continuation of another work, one not read by the potential buyer, sales would have been adversely affected. This would explain the change in the pseudonyms and the changes in the figures' names. In the *Winternächte* they are mostly of Romance origin (the novel purports to be a translation of a sixty-year-old manuscript!),[13] whereas in the sequel the characters' names are German. At the same time, the publisher probably wished to exploit the interest of those who had read the *Winternächte* and therefore gave the sequel an eye-catching, linking title.

Let us turn to the action of the two novels. *Winternächte* opens *in medias res* with a mystery that is explained piecemeal. "It was about midnight when I found myself freed outside the castle where I had endured a thousand uncertainties of imprisonment."[14] The speaker is the narrator, Zendorio, a wandering student "with little wealth but a good name" who had been imprisoned without explanation. Continuing his journey, he comes to the castle of a young nobleman named Isidoro and tells his story. At that point he learns why he had been incarcerated. While staying at an inn, Zendorio had discovered that his clothes had been stolen. Having donned the clothing left in place of his own, he had set out again for the university, whereupon he had been seized and locked in a dungeon. It all turns out to be a case of mistaken identity: Isidoro, who loves the infamous Veronia, had been pursued by her outraged husband and had saved himself by exchanging clothes with Zendorio. Out of gratitude, and because he gets on well with the student, Isidoro invites him to stay at his castle. In this way Zendorio moves into a social circle made up of persons of the lesser nobility, a squirearchy with little interest in the city or court whose amusements are storytelling, hunting, carousing, and playing practical jokes on one another and on the peasants.

At one of several boisterous parties that take up significant portions of the *Winternächte*, Zendorio meets the noblewoman Caspia and is strongly attracted to her in spite of the class barrier between them. But in the course of the party he becomes so inebriated that he dances around wearing nothing but his soiled nightshirt. The next day he leaves in shame, thinking himself disgraced. He walks aimlessly for several days, stopping for one night at the home of a minister, then arriving, by a wild coincidence characteristic of the work, at the castle of Caspia. He is so filthy from travel that she fails to recognize him and asks his advice—since he is a student—on a personal matter. She reveals that she has fallen in love with a man named Zendorio. Who could be happier than our young hero, especially when, having revealed his identity, Caspia says she can have a patent of nobility conferred on him. But then fate again intervenes when Zendorio's father appears and says he is a skinner,[15] one of the lowest of all occupations. Once again humiliated, Zendorio runs away, planning to become a soldier. After six months of wandering he accidentally meets Isidoro, who tells him that his father is actually Monsieur Pilemann, a nobleman who had foolishly had his son brought up by others because of his superstitiousness: gypsy fortunetellers had told him that if he had his son raised by peasants, the boy would become a general by the time he was eighteen. The "skinner" who interrupted Zendorio's planned marriage was actually M. Pilemann in disguise, and Zendorio had rushed off before his father could reveal the story of his origin. Caspia still loves Zendorio, Isidoro says, and will welcome him back, but a few days later, when they stop at an inn near her castle, they learn that she has died.

Zendorio finds recent events in his life a perfect illustration of how man is buffeted by the fickle winds of fortune.[16] He becomes a hermit, lives for a time in an isolated forest, and is rescued by hunters as he is about to be attacked by wolves. Zendorio learns that they are hunting game for the wedding feast of Caspia and Faustus, another suitor. Caspia, it turns out, is alive (a relative by the same name had died), but, believing Zendorio to be dead, she has accepted another bid for her hand. At the banquet Zendorio makes a dramatic appearance, and Faustus storms out. There is a merry marriage celebration, with games and storytelling involving both men and women. Ludwig alternately amuses and shocks the women in the group with his wit and propensity for off-color jokes. He has learned about the world not in university lectures but from the perusal of novels and "satires." The women are witty and give a good accounting of themselves in their life stories but are not portrayed as equal partners in the discussions, or indeed as the intellectual match of men. The group disperses to various castles.

Zendorio is enjoying his new status as a responsible landowner. He reports that the group of friends urged him to write this chronicle, a task which he takes seriously. The events are therefore recorded sometime after they have occurred, in the manner of most picaresque novels. But Zendorio's life, particularly in Book Five (of Six), is by no means picaresque: he administers the estate prudently and treats his tenants justly. A huntsman named Ergasto appears at the castle and reveals that he is the man who freed Zendorio at the beginning of the novel, that he was in the employ of Veronia, and that he, Ergasto, is Isidoro's brother. Ergasto speaks of Veronia at length, and characterizes her as a monster who has a liking only for "nasty fellows." She is one of those moral villainesses familiar to us from Beer's antifeminist novels. Even Zendorio's own servant, Jost, who tells his history, was involved with Veronia when he was eight and she thirteen!

There are more weddings and pleasant evenings of conversation, and Zendorio spends part of the winter in singing and composition. Beer ties up the loose ends of the plot with the result that virtually every figure turns out to be in some way connected with all the others. Ergasto marries, and on the way home from the celebration Zendorio meets a young monk: it is the Irishman, who instead of marrying has renounced the world. On arriving at his castle Zendorio finds that Caspia has given birth to their first child. At the conclusion of the *Winternächte* the noblemen celebrate the marriage of Jost. The feast becomes a debauch, and on awakening the next morning to the admonitions of the Irishman, they return to their castles with the resolution to change their ways. Thus ends the novel.

The *Sommer-Täge* reintroduces types familiar to us from the *Winternächte*, as mentioned. There are also a few new figures, most of them peripheral, such as the "lawyer of Ollingen," and one significant one, the villain, "Barthel of the Heath." The introduction reveals that the noblemen sought various ways to amuse themselves in the summer heat—riding, jousting, playing music together in the shade of the trees—but none of these activities is satisfying, and they decide to "ban, for a time, worldly joy from our hearts" and "to go into the cool and shadowy forests and to see how the hermit's life would taste."[17] In the *Sommer-Täge* it is the "pious Friderich," the Scot, who sways them to this decision, which is a spontaneous, almost playful one. Their stay in the forest is brief; they have a reunion and relate their various experiences.

Motifs of the courtly or adventure novel similar to those found in the *Verliebte Oesterreicher* surface in the second book in the form of repeated armed clashes between a nobleman turned robber-captain, Barthel, and Friderich and his friends. Friderich is in love with the beautiful and virtuous Amalia, but Barthel is out to win her for himself by force or trickery. Much of the novel's action revolves around this conflict. In other ways the sequel closely resembles its predecessor, but there are signs of change in the lives of the figures: some of the noblemen's wives become pregnant, Wolffgang's father and child die the same day, and the circle gradually drifts apart, Philipp going to court, others joining the army or traveling to Italy. The narrator finds his interests in his own castle, in the persons of the old soldier Krachwedel, who served under Wallenstein and who so pleases Wolffgang with his stories that he is kept on; in Jäckel, the page; and in his conceited scribe or secretary. A traveling student joins and complements the group.

In the meantime, Wolffgang has fallen in love with Lisel, a neighboring woman of noble family, while his first wife, Sophia, is suddenly aged and dies, arbitrarily jerked from the stage by Beer. But when Wolffgang marries Lisel he soon sees the folly of his action. She is lazy, bibulous, overbearing, and unfaithful. After a time, having served Beer's didactic purpose, she too dies, and Wolffgang increasingly devotes himself to the *vita contemplativa*. He again dons the hermit's garb and goes into the mountains. But he is not forced to rely entirely on his own woodcraft to survive: his page brings supplies and food. Later, he succeeds in renouncing the victuals from the castle and grows so thin as to be hardly recognizable. He meditates, reads devotional literature, and prays. He even becomes an object of curiosity and is forced to move to a more remote location. By coincidence, two of his friends happen on his hut—having been robbed in an inn on the way back from Italy—and there is a joyous reunion. All three return to Wolffgang's castle for a celebration, but now the narrator too seems suddenly aged: he is in his sixties and becoming ever more otherworldly, he returns to his hermitage. There he accidentally discovers that old Krachwedel, although twenty-nine years his senior, is his long-lost brother Emanuel.

In the meantime, Philipp has deserted the court, the lawyer has died, Wilhelm lives a life of asceticism, Friderich is living happily with his wife, Amalia (Barthel of the Heath having long before been skewered in combat), and the student is administering a castle entrusted to him by Wolffgang. The narrator thinks increasingly of his eternal soul, quoting from the works of Thomas à Kempis (1380–1471), part of whose *Imitation of Christ* he has translated into German. When he concludes the work it is winter, and he is living frugally in his tower room, occasionally having his servants perform a comedy for him. But he constantly thinks of Thomas à Kempis's renunciation of the world and is prepared for "sweet eternity, thou most pleasant hope of my soul."[18]

Throughout the novel, Zendorio acts as a chronicler of occurrences he holds to be of moral significance and exemplary value.

I've excoriated myself in several episodes and told my own story with the rest. On these winter nights I've walked ahead through the snow so that those whom

I met here and there might follow more easily, on a path, so to speak. [. . .] This story wasn't written on a whim, but because I promised to describe everything that happened to me and to those I knew. [. . .] I would have gladly given this arduous task to the Irishman or someone else, but because they practically forced me to do it I had all the better reason to tell things just the way they happened.[19]

Thus Beer seeks, and not just playfully, to represent the action of the novel as fact. But he carries out his plan inconsistently or only sporadically, for the existence of the narrator-chronicler (who must be distinguished from the narrator-actor) is alluded to only very rarely. The chronicler surfaces only when the novel becomes contemplative,[20] and the reader tends to forget or discount the fiction that the tale had been set down as a chronicle. One is tempted to say that Beer too lost sight of his narrative technique over long stretches of the work, since he tells the story from the standpoint of Zendorio-Wolffgang, describing events in the order and manner in which the narrator-author experiences them. But the narrator-chronicler, or narrator-author, scarcely ever anticipates events—does not write, for instance, "Little did I know what lay in store for me at Veronia's castle"—but allows the narrator-actor to tell his story from his own limited viewpoint. The best example of this technique of delayed revelation is Beer's treatment of the mysterious set of circumstances at the outset of the novel. Zendorio is imprisoned without reason, is literally in the dark. We learn the reason for his arrest shortly thereafter from Isidoro, but it is only much later that we hear a complete version of the event from the huntsman Ergasto.[21] It is interesting that the narrator-chronicler makes no effort either to enlighten the reader or to enhance the literary effect of the mystery by dropping hints as to its solution. In short, while the narrator generally employs the past tense, "the story unfolds as if he does not always command an unobstructed view of the entire proceedings, as if he cannot look ahead to give an indication of future developments, but must let the story take its own natural course."[22] Beer only twice allows the narrator-chronicler to glance into the future, once when Zendorio ironically remarks that while he is not a member of the nobility, he is of "such a race as will astonish" the reader,[23] a reference to the revelation some twenty pages later that he is apparently a skinner's son. But this is an odd anticipation since it turns out that he actually *is* a nobleman. One therefore wonders if this is a genuine literary anticipation interjected by the narrator-chronicler[24] or one supplied by the narrator-actor, much as if he were telling a story. One cannot say that Beer simply lost sight of the fact that the story was presumably written down after the events described have occurred, because it is pointed out that Zendorio writes his narrative piecemeal.[25] Hence, anticipations of future events might be conceived to be limited to the scope of a particular segment of the novel. A genuine anticipation of the "chronicler" occurs when Wolffgang refers to a strange affinity he feels for Krachwedel, "for reasons that the reader will later understand," and some years and hundreds of pages later we learn that the two are brothers.

In short, the role of the primary and secondary narrator is more complex than is immediately apparent. While Beer's primary narrator makes very little use of his power to look ahead, there are numerous secondary anticipations voiced by figures within the story.[26] Their presence suggests that Beer paid greater attention than was his wont to the structure of the Willenhag novels.

Characterization obviously plays a secondary role to plot in the Willenhag novels. Figures are "typed" according to social class. There are two basic groups of characters: the country nobility, and the peasants or poor wandering figures such as musicians, soldiers, and students. The representatives of the latter group generally work for a time at a castle and then continue their wanderings. But within each social group many figures are so similar as almost to be interchangeable: one thinks, for instance, of the recurring foul-mouthed female servants. The range of personalities is therefore limited; Beer's imaginativeness lies more in the manipulation of events, in the variation on similar themes, than in delineation of character. His creation of complex links among figures coming from the most disparate backgrounds, his emphasis on incident, are the primary characteristics of the Willenhag novels. Another, also demonstrating Beer's preoccupation with event, is the technique of delayed revelation. And he frequently combines mystery and humor in a unique manner. I have already mentioned Zendorio's mysterious arrest, and there are even more bizarre examples: Zendorio finds a man hanging from a tree, rushes to his aid, but is warned away by an accomplice concealed in a hollow tree.[27] It is only much later that the "hanging" is revealed to be a hoax.

With all his attention to intricate connections among his figures Beer was careless—perhaps deliberately so—in the treatment of time and the ages of his characters.[28] The span of the action in the two novels is about forty-two years altogether, but exact dates and numbers are rarely given. Willenhag is presumably around sixty-two at the conclusion of the *Sommer-Täge*, which would mean that Krachwedel is ninety-one. At this point we learn that the old warrior has a four-year-old son! When Sophia, Wolffgang's first wife, dies, she is seventy-two, an age that is out of kilter with her husband's, which is about fifty. It is difficult to say whether Beer merely overlooked these inconsistencies or was twitting his audience.

Beer provides few precise dates, but there are references to historical events that enable us to determine within a year or two the dates of certain episodes. For instance, in the *Winternächte* Isidoro's mother mentions the battle of Wittstock, which took place on 4 October 1632, and says that since the battle about thirty-two years have passed. She therefore must be speaking in 1664 or 1665.[29] And in the *Sommer-Täge*, at the age of eighty to ninety, Krachwedel tells of the battle of Stadtlohn,[30] allowing us to place the time of that portion of the novel in the 1680s. It is clear that Beer was not intent on precisely dating the events, but that he set the action roughly in a time corresponding to his own. With some exceptions, such as Krachwedel, the figures are therefore about a generation younger than Simplicissimus.

As in most novels—one thinks particularly of Mann's *The Magic Mountain*—there are wide variations between elapsed time in the narrative and between the number of pages devoted to like periods of time.[31] That is, while each book has approximately the same number of pages, the time covered varies from two days and nights in Book II of the *Winternächte*, with its many "flashbacks," to many years in Books IV to VI of the *Sommer-Täge*. The first novel describes events of two to three years, the second those of around forty years. Beer is clearly intent on highlighting certain events, usually the festivities of the noblemen, into which frame are then placed secondary anecdotes or life histories that often relate to the mainstream of the narrative.

Nor is Beer intent on specifically fixing the events of the work geographically. As in the *Verliebte Oesterreicher*, actual place names occur, and many of these are found in the Attergau, as Alewyn has pointed out, although some are invented. The locations of the noblemen's castles and their distance from one another are not precisely described. In short, the geographical picture is somewhat cloudier than Alewyn found it.[32] The one detailed topographical description, one particularly singled out by Alewyn as an example of the specificity and realism of the novels, describes in glowing colors a region—upper Austria—unrelated to the main action of the novels. In other words, it appears rather unmotivated and is surely to be chalked up to Beer's local patriotism.[33] Our author is interested in the portrayal of events, not of topography. He evokes a landscape that vaguely suggests the Attergau, his birthplace, yet Zendorio says his castle is not far from the Rhine! In this work, space is a means to an end, a fictional, arbitrary landscape.

In the last two decades a debate over the meaning and usefulness of the term realism has been raging and will doubtless continue to do so. In Beer studies the question takes on particular significance since Alewyn claimed an unprecedented realism for Beer's novels, holding him in this respect to be superior to Grimmelshausen, whose *Simplicissimus* he termed "naturalistic," by which he meant contrived, exaggerated. His perception of Beer as a writer uniquely in touch with reality has fallen into disfavor in recent years, as did his characterization of Grimmelshausen as a naturalistic writer whose descriptions, far from being realistic, are filled with exaggeration and caricature.[34] Of Beer, on the other hand, he writes: "Such a pure and rich relationship to reality is by no means typical of the Baroque; on the contrary, it distinguishes Beer completely from all contemporary and previous writers, above all from that man of great imagination, Grimmelshausen."[35]

Alewyn then provides his own conception of realism, since, as he points out, about the only aspect of Grimmelshausen's works agreed upon by scholars of the time was that the Simplician novels were "realistic." Alewyn writes that if one actually analyzes Grimmelshausen's descriptions one will find that this vaunted realism is lacking. Not only is there a singular lack of detail in descriptive passages, but one can learn little about life in the city, on the farm, or in the family in the seventeenth century from a reading of *Simplicissimus*. What the author in fact describes are abnormal conditions: war and the picaresque existence. Setting is only described in sufficient detail to provide a background for the action; the contours are not sharp.[36] Alewyn claims that Grimmelshausen's descriptions are not realistic and singles out his description of the battle of Wittstock; he compares its "subjectivity" with a passage from Beer's *Jucundus Jucundissimus*, which does indeed contain an amazing wealth of information.

Understandably, many Grimmelshausen scholars disagree with Alewyn's hypothesis and point to the presence of numerous passages in Grimmelshausen's novels that correspond to Alewyn's definition of realism and to passages in Beer's novels that can be called "naturalistic" in Alewyn's sense.[37] And there are several novels by Beer which provide only the scantiest description of milieu, barely enough to furnish a background for the action—which is precisely what Alewyn saw in Grimmelshausen's novels. There is no question, then, that Alewyn's thesis must be revised considerably.

But this is only one problem. A much broader one concerns the very meaning of the term "realism." On the one extreme, it is carelessly used by some virtually to mean "naturalistic" as the word is applied to literature of the late nineteenth century. Thus, one reads of a "realistic" (i.e., brutal, frank) film. The fuzzy use of the word is comparable to the abuse of the word "romantic." At the other extreme, the realism controversy has given rise to extremely convoluted definitions that seem to signal the revival of neoscholastic hairsplitting.

Stated simply, the realistic style tends to portray events in a manner that closely corresponds to most persons' perception of similar events. The actions described are consonant with those we have known to have occurred; the style is consistent with the situation and social status of the speakers. Realism tends to provide a fully described background for the action of the novel and tends to avoid stylized or dreamlike methods of portrayal. It is in the general sense that Alewyn understood realism and that I will use the term in the following pages.

Gerhard Fricke's 1933 review of Alewyn's book on Beer contained the first criticism of Alewyn's characterization of Beer as a realist, pointing to all the improbabilities, coincidences, redundancies, improbable disguises, and mistaken identities in Beer's novels. But this does not negate the realistic tendency in these works. One must try to see through seventeenth-century eyes: ghosts were reality to Beer and to most of his generation. Admittedly, he makes use of fantastic, magical settings in some of his earlier novels, but there is no such tendency in the Willenhag novels. On the contrary, it is clear that Beer was attempting to write works that reflect the real world because—and one is inclined to accept the sincerity of the reason he gives—such works would have greater moral effect on the reader. And that is why, according to one of the work's figures, Frau von Pockau, it is justified to include crude ingredients in a story:

Some time ago I read in many books a lot of lofty and mighty love-stories, but they were tales that could not have happened. And so the time I spent reading such writings was ill-spent because there was no way to make use of what I found in the book. But the things that happened to Ludwig in his youth still occur a thousand-fold and particularly among us. I therefore consider them far more important than those [courtly novels] because they could happen to us and we have the opportunity to find in them lessons we can use in avoiding vice.

The stories from Ludwig's youth referred to include illicit love affairs and considerable vulgarity. Beer shrewdly chooses to have a woman justify his realism, although it is difficult to see why Ludwig's life story would be of particular relevance to country nobility. More consistent with Beer's standpoint is Frau von Pockau's own story of the evil consequences of reading idealized literature. As a girl she had read a story about a

Turkish princess with most discriminating tastes in suitors. She took the fictional figure as a model, turning down all her suitors—with the result that she ceased to have any. She now perceives a real contemporary problem among middle-class women who were, or are, enamored of fantastic or idealistic literature. The problem was not limited to women: the Irishman relates that in his youth he was an avid reader of tales of chivalry that grievously misled him about the true nature of life.[42]

One is inclined to agree with Alewyn[43] that, at least in the Willenhag novels, Beer had an eye for detail unusual in his time. As a portrayal of the rural nobility of the seventeenth century, the Willenhag novels are significant literary documents. One sees the world of the noblemen with great clarity; one meets the gatekeeper, the secretary, the stableboy or hunter, the cooks and servants. To be sure, the servants tend to be types, but some of them, particularly those who tell their life histories, are characterized at least as sensitively as most of the noblemen. One naturally cannot know how accurate Beer's portrayal of this small world is. There is no evidence that he actually moved in the circles of the Upper Austrian nobility while he lived in St. Georgen; in all likelihood, he was merely on the periphery. In later life, he was on a friendly footing with many noblemen at the Weissenfels court, and it may be that there is in the work as much of that court's propensity for festivity and the martial arts as of Upper Austria.

There can be no question of the presence of a strong autobiographical tendency in the work: the author tells us as much in "The Author to His Book," a poem preceding Chapter 1 of the *Winternächte*:

> You friends, who still live as my joy and consolation,
> Accept this, my work, for your service.
> I know no way to repay you save through this book,
> In which you can recognize me, and I you.[44]

From what we know about Beer's personality, his unconventionality, his gregariousness, it is easy to see him not only in Zendorio-Wolffgang, but also in Ludwig and other figures. It is no contradiction to say that we find traits of Beer in the pious Irishman as well, for it has become clear in our study of the man and his works that conflicting and probably disturbing tendencies of hedonism and asceticism were present in his psyche. A related point is the constantly recurring motif of the poor, often-abused boy who rises to a position of prominence or turns out to be of noble parentage. This might even be called the predominant motif in

Beer's novels. There can be no doubt that the author was thinking not only of Grimmelshausen's Simplicius figure but also of his own deprived youth and his rise to a relatively high social and financial status.[45]

Beer's realism is not that of the nineteenth century. Alewyn points out that he portrays action realistically but attempts to analyze the personalities of even the chief figures to an extent no greater than Grimmelshausen. There is a somewhat weak attempt at differentiation of individuality through brief characterizations—somewhat in the manner of the *Canterbury Tales*—in the opening of the *Sommer-Täge*, where the main figures are introduced.[46]

Beer does attempt to explore depths of emotion; his portrayals are often convincing and occasionally moving, even if they have little subtlety. Perhaps the most striking example occurs when Zendorio, having become intoxicated at a banquet, humiliates himself before the entire assemblage. He rides off the next day in dire mental anguish: "In that frame of mind I left the castle and had the strangest emotions; I'd have given a finger from my hand never to have joined or even set eyes on this group."[47] His sudden departure causes Caspia to fall ill, and it is even thought that she had died of that characteristic malady of the age, melancholy. It is at this point that we find what is perhaps Beer's most convincing depiction of emotion:

I had only a sister [not otherwise mentioned] of fifteen [. . .] and she consoled me as best she could at her age, not knowing what terrible grief one felt at the loss of something both from one's hopes and possession.
My father himself grieved with me. He wept and for my sake acted more hurt than I would have expected. [. . .] So I locked myself in my room and wept all alone, without consolation or hope, the most forlorn person under the sun."[48]

Alewyn and other have remarked on Beer's eye for description of action. His descriptions of dancing, fencing, playing musical instruments, gestures, and the like are sometimes unusually detailed, even mannered. Here, for instance, a picture of Ludwig's reactions when reunited with Zendorio:

Hereupon he led me up a stone stairway of eight steps [!], and there I sat down with him in a little room where I told him how I'd lived and in what misery the time had passed. Now he jumped up, now he sat down again, so much was he affected by my story. He wrung his hands, swung them now and again over his head, then placed them on his stomach, and then grasped me with both his arms [. . .].[49]

Beer is skillful at the depiction of scenes at table or storytelling. The conversations among the noblemen and ladies, and the shock of the latter at Ludwig's or Philipp's coarseness, probably accurately reflect the discourses the author heard at the Weissenfels court or possibly in lower social circles. The conversations are not as witty and learned as those concocted by Harsdörffer, but they have a more realistic ring. This is so not only because of the realistic style and subject matter of the stories told by the group, but also because Beer frequently causes the "frame" of the story to intrude upon the story being recounted. For instance, a servant announces that dinner is ready, but the circle is so engrossed with the tale being told (and so, presumably, is the reader) that the servant is instructed to delay the meal by fifteen minutes.[50] And the realism of the conversations is heightened by Ludwig's knack for tantalizing his audience by leaving out the spiciest parts of the tales but nonetheless alluding to them.

In summary, Beer claims that he wished his novels to exert a moral influence on the reader, and we have no reason to doubt him. He was repelled by the artificial and pretentious, whether it be in matters of clothing, speech, or literary style. In contrast to the *Verliebte Oesterreicher*, the Willenhag novels are written in the style he was accustomed to using and hearing. The freshness and vitality of the language of these novels reinforce the impression that much of what we read in the work, although transposed and rearranged, does indeed represent a truthful chronicle.

It is inevitable in a work the length of the Willenhag novels that Beer should have expressed, consciously and unconsciously, some of his basic social and religious views. Of central importance is the author's treatment of the eremitic life and the theme of friendship. Certain of Ludwig's remarks are also particularly revealing, as will be shown.

As we have seen, the theme of the eremitic life recurs in this work, as it had, with painful regularity, in the *Weltkucker*. Earlier I mentioned the hollow ring of this motif in Beer's first novel, and in the Willenhag novels we also detect little genuine religiosity.[51] Alewyn points out that in Beer the hermit's life has been secularized and no longer represents religious asceticism, as had Grimmelshausen's *Simplicissimus*. In fact, there is something playful in the way Wolffgang and his friends embark upon their experimentations with the simple life. At the beginning of the *Sommer-Täge* their choice of the hermit's existence is only one of several possibilities, others being jousting or the telling of tales.[52] Alewyn likens their elaborate preparations (the hermit clothing has to be tailored, provisions provided) with that notorious artifice of the aristocracy, the bucolic shepherd's life, as it was used in pastoral literature and indeed played out at court.[53] The hermit's life had become a kind of game.[54] Thus it may be true that the hermit is no longer central to the novels. But Beer's attitude toward this popular motif—one that fascinated his contemporaries and that therefore had a certain literary market value—is important for what it tells us about Beer. His protagonists toy so frequently with the idea of taking up the hermit's existence that one must conclude he too found a certain fascination in it and did not merely use the motif to express a philosophical position. While it can reasonably be argued that Beer rejects altogether the concept of a hermit's existence[55] (whatever that metaphor may have implied to him), since several figures in effect say that it is an unnatural withdrawal, I feel that he was seriously drawn to such a way of life (priest? scholar?) at some point in his career. Beer's attitude toward the hermit metaphor is therefore ambivalent. This ambivalence is found not only in the characters' initial desire to take up a lonely existence, for whatever reason—grief at the death of Caspia, remorse after the excesses of a celebration—and their subsequent distaste for it, but also in the contradiction between the espousal of an active, practical life in some passages and the *vita contemplativa* in others. In his introductory poem, "Author to His Book," Beer writes:

> Go to those, to whom I cannot go,
> My book, and say that I still live full of fire,
> And say that my life will consist in such flames
> Until I say farewell to this idle world.[56]

The poem shows its author's pride in his own drive and verve. It hardly seems consonant with the total renunciation of human society attempted by Zendorio, or even with the concluding situation in the *Sommer-Täge*, when Wolffgang lives a gentle form of the hermit's life that allows him in the winter to return to the comforts of his castle. It may be that Beer's point was that withdrawal from life is a mistake and self-deception for most persons—they end up eating roots and getting the stomach-ache— but proper and good for others, or that a gradual withdrawal from worldly matters is not unnatural as one grows older.[57] But none of these explanations fully accounts for the protagonist's wild swings from sensual excess to remorse and pious resolve. One may hazard a guess that these unresolved conflicts reflect Beer's personal experiences and his own inability as a young man of twenty-eight to reconcile the religious principles—so sternly and unceasingly inculcated in him—with his strong sensual drives. His figures attempt through reason—ego versus id, one might say —rather more than through God to direct their drives into proper and useful channels, but fall into the same traps again and again. All the friends—who clearly represent various aspects of Beer's personality—reflect their creator's own experience: most men are doomed to sin by their animal origin, or by the "Fall," as Beer's age saw it.

The role of friendship is central to the moral and intellectual self-improvement for which all the members of the circle strive. It is not restricted to the nobility. There is also friendship between master and page, where social distance is bridged by camaraderie, and between mentor and young man. While the friendship between members of the aristocratic group never quite attains the sentimentality found in the friendship between Simplicissimus and Herzbruder, it is sincere and cordial. This sort of friendship stands in stark contrast to the hypocrisy of the court, and is linked with Beer's frequent praise of country life over that at court and in the city.[58] Although the fact is often obscured by the welter of detail in the work, the friends encourage one another to follow the path of virtue. I concede that they are, sometimes, self-indulgent, lazy, even immoral, and they have nothing in the way of a program for improvement of secular institutions. Their disdain for the court and city, for virtually all the professions (lawyer, merchant, priest), leaves the circle open to the charge that it is capable only of criticizing abuses of the time without presenting its own practical ethical system. The actions of the novels' figures refute this charge more than do their words. Wolffgang's concern for the proper administration of his estates is documented in great detail and illustrates the point. But there are words, too, that show the presence of a coherent practical philosophy and which clearly represent Beer's own views. One such passage, a speech by Ludwig, reads:

"The satirical writings and other novels gave me the best instruction in all matters, and I considered them much more useful and necessary than the logic and all the definitions, because I saw that scholars were much less in agreement with one another than the satirists [. . .]. [Here he lists works he read, including Buchholtz's *Hercules*, Sidney's *Arcadia*, Moscherosch's *Gesichte Philanders von Sittewald*, Barclay's *Argenis*, Sorel's *Francion*, Grimmelshausen's *Simplicissimus*, works by Harsdörffer, by Erasmus Francisci, Eberhard Happel, all the volumes of the *Amadís*, as well as scholarly works.] But I say that by reading them I gained greater rhetorical skill than I could have got from a professor in twelve months. [. . .] I saw, as though I were in a theater, how things happen in this world [. . .]. Because of that I became half a *Politicus*, for things happened to me just as they'd happened to others in books, and I used their methods to great advantage in my life.

"For definitions don't mean much to me, and it's far more useful to me to know how and when to plow the field, to sow the grain, to cut the hay, shake the apple trees, to fatten the pigs, wean the calves, to fell wood, to manage the servants, than it would be if I were a highfalutin Ph.D. And my barns look far more glorious filled with grain than [they would] filled with books. And for that reason I live with great pleasure in my freedom which I have [always] held in high esteem, so that I've never wanted to submit myself to the opinion of a philosopher. [He goes on to say he has never learned the rules of oratory, but wagers he could more than hold his own with a scholar. He speaks further of his broad knowledge of agriculture.] Oh, there's nothing foolish about farming—it requires as much or more effort than philosophy. One considers the peasants dumb because they don't bow and scrape like today's trendy set does, but in their own profession they are just as much doctors as we in our sciences."[59]

This somewhat anti-intellectual speech of Ludwig reveals in my view the full extent of Beer's pragmatism. There is no doubt that Ludwig's sympathy for the peasant as well as his contempt for the theoretician-scholar comes from Beer's heart.

Finally, we think it is obvious that there is something that smacks of wishful thinking in this picture of a fun-loving yet well-intentioned circle of noblemen.[60] Beer created a society to which he would have liked to belong; he placed it in an isolated, stable rural setting not only because of his warm feelings for Upper Austria, but in order to portray a microcosm whose values are independent of those of corrupt, conventional society and whose judicial rights are only minimally restricted.[61] In such a world Beer could not only indulge his predilection for telling tales of a humorous, outrageous nature, but could also treat a subject that must have obsessed him: sin, and subsequent remorse and repentance.

Chapter Six
Conclusion

K.G. Knight points out that Beer thought of himself primarily as a musician and composer, not as a novelist.[1] This observation is unquestionably true, since Beer repeatedly stresses the nobility of music and the effort and time required to attain musical proficiency. He took the art of writing less seriously, as he states in the forewords of several works. Other clues that Beer did not exert his energies and talent to their full extent in his novels are that, while he allowed his name to appear on the title pages of his theoretical works on music and on those of the polemics defending it against fundamentalist zealotry, all his novels appeared anonymously or under various pseudonyms. Then there is the rumor reported by Adlung that in later life Beer regretted having published his satires at all,[2] as well as the facts that there is not a single allusion to the novels in Beer's diary and that he wrote most if not all his novels in the period from 1677 to 1685, between the ages of twenty-two and thirty. Nothing is more obvious than that the twenty-one novels were written at white-hot speed. Even Richard Alewyn, who understandably felt a special warmth for the works of the long-neglected author, conceded that structurally the novels of Beer are episodic and show little evidence of careful planning. Even his best novels do not approach the structural consistency and symmetry of Grimmelshausen's *Simplicissimus*, whose first five books Scholte likened to the five acts of a classical tragedy.[3] In other words, what Beer achieved in his fiction came about in a somewhat improvised, offhand way, as writing was a kind of profitable hobby for him.

And yet Beer's achievement is astonishing. In the span of eight years he wrote at least nineteen novels, some in two or more parts, and these were years when he was engaged in university study, composition, the search for a suitable position in Regensburg or Halle, courtship, marriage and fatherhood, the move to the court at Weissenfels, and the assumption of new and demanding duties there. Admittedly, much that he wrote, particularly the antifeminist satires, is harsh, abstract, repetitive, and lifeless, devoid of interest for the modern taste. His picaresque novels, on the other hand, are distinguished by their ingenuity and capricious humor, and Beer's most mature work, the Willenhag novels, demonstrates skill in the delineation of character unusual for the age and in the creation of a stable, credible world possessing what Alewyn called epic breadth. While this work lacks the depth of feeling found in passages of *Simplicissimus*, its main figures have sharply and consistently differentiated personalities. Ludwig-Philipp's bluff heartiness and his predilection for the off-color pun or *double entendre* and the Irishman-Scot's pious otherworldliness mark the extremes of personality in the circle of friends. Wolffgang's character emerges very gradually in the course of the *Sommer-Täge*, and one finds not only the practicality of a landowner and farmer but also a sensitivity, even sentimentality of which his thicker-skinned friends are incapable. In short, I feel that Beer was more adept at characterization than Alewyn allows. Alewyn implies that Beer's "realism" is to be equated with his importance as a novelist,[4] a conclusion I cannot share. While one cannot dispute the strong realistic tendency of such works as *Jucundus Jucundissimus* and the Willenhag novels, it may be that Beer's greatest literary strength resides in his whimsical humor, which has been documented in detail in the preceding chapters, and in his fantasy and imaginativeness. Who but Beer, for instance, could have concocted the story of a tightrope walker who was unable to take up the trumpet because he had lost his front teeth in a freak accident? His father, a city musician and a smallish man, had been bowled over by a gust of wind while playing atop the city tower, and his trumpet had knocked out the boy's teeth.[5] And consider the fancifully described procession of secretaries in the *Verkehrte Staats-Mann*, the allegorical kitchen utensils in the *Bratenwender*, or the bizarre visions of Ludwig—of all people—in the *Winternächte*. Bedridden with a six-week fever he hallucinates, seeing "hundreds of pairs of patched, torn, and ragged stockings which I mended with my writing materials, and they honored me in return with an old wig. [. . .] I tore my grammar into a thousand little pieces and I had these pieces of paper roasted on a skewer and ate them like hens. Then came a big cooking-fork with [musical] strings on it which I played on for over four hours. [. . .] I thought everyone who visited me during that illness to be knapsacks, feather-dusters, spires, hazelnuts, quill-pens, bench-legs, and cow-tails [. . .]."[6] Alewyn is probably correct when he writes that Beer was the "author of the most humorous and whimsical books of his century."[7]

Scholarly opinion today tends to regard Beer's works with less favor than did Alewyn. It is conceded that Beer was a gifted writer who flouted conventions of genre and verisimilitude when to do so served his purposes. He was an experimenter, in the literary vanguard in many respects—for instance, in his rejection of the overladen, flowery style.

Certainly, his Willenhag novels deserve mention among the best examples of humoristic German literature. But his works have had, thus
far, almost no resonance outside German-speaking countries, and even
within these countries they seem to have had little impact. But this
circumstance may, in part, be an accident of fate, since Beer was
"discovered" only relatively recently; moreover, the degree of his influence on German letters is irrelevant to the issue of his literary rank. After
all, Weise's *Drei Ertz-Narren* went through ten editions by 1710 and was
immensely influential, but it is inferior to most of Beer's novels. If one
charitably disregards the majority of his political novels as commercial
speculations, Beer stands out as one of the most imaginative novelists of
the century in Germany. While Beer was not the literary equal of
Grimmelshausen, he was his worthy successor.

Notes and References

Chapter One

1. Richard Alewyn, *Johann Beer* (Leipzig, 1932). Henceforth cited as Alewyn, *Beer*. Arnold Hirsch discovered three of Beer's novels (cf. Alewyn, *Beer*, p. ix.).

2. *Johann Beer. Sein Leben, von ihm selbst erzählt.* (Göttingen, 1965). Henceforth cited as *Diary*.

3. It still serves as the village inn.

4. See Fritz Habeck, *Der verliebte Österreicher oder Johannes Beer* (Graz: Stiasny, 1961), pp. 19ff. This work includes excerpts from the *Welt-Kucker*, longish portions of the *Verliebter Österreicher*, and Habeck's informal and breezy but informative biography of Beer.

5. Johann Mattheson, *Grundlage einer Ehrenpforte* [. . .] (Hamburg, 1740), pp. 14f. Mattheson's work was the source for most musical lexicons of the eighteenth and nineteenth centuries and also a chief source for the biography of Beer in a standard biographical work, *Allgemeine Deutsche Biographie*. It is interesting that Mattheson knew Beer to be the author of several novels that had appeared pseudonymously; Mattheson was struck by the fact that "his style betrays him quite sufficiently" (p. 16).

6. Quoted in the original in my introduction to Johann Beer, *Der verliebte Oesterreicher* (Bern and Frankfurt, 1978), *Nachdrucke deutscher Literatur des 17. Jahrhunderts*, pp. 17f.

7. For the reconstruction of this feud see Manfred Kremer, "Der Kantor im Werke Johann Beers," *Modern Language Notes* 88 (1973):1023−29.

8. Probably a real person; Beer mentions a concertmaster named Mylius in his diary, p. 26 (Schmiedecke ed.).

9. *Ritter Spiridon*, pp. a2^v−a3^r.

10. *Diary*, p. 19. He may have attended the university in Altdorf as early as 1675, as he is listed in the *Matrikel der Universität Altdorf*, 12:381, under that year. See Harold Jantz, "German Baroque Literature," *Modern Language Notes* 57 (1962):351.

11. See my foreword to *Der verliebte Oesterreicher*, p. 21.

12. *Diary*, p. 21.

13. See Alewyn, *Beer*, p. 43.

14. Friedrich Gerhardt, *Schloss und Schloss-Kirche zu Weissenfels* (Weissenfels, 1898), pp. 49f.

15. See Arno Werner, *Städtische und fürstliche Musikpflege in Weissenfels* (Leipzig, 1911), p. 65.

16. *Musicalische Discurse* (Nuremberg: Monath, 1719), p. 21.

17. It should be pointed out that Beer's diary is largely retrospective, and that therefore the earlier portions are quite brief and sketchy in comparison

to those that were written after 1690, when apparently the notations were begun.

18. The term "novel" will be used without quotation marks henceforth but with the understanding that the idea of the "novel" as a genre had not yet gelled. The German word for novel, a loan word from the French, *roman* or *romain*, was seldom used by Beer and by few of his contemporaries. The title-pages of his novels use such terms as *Geschicht* ("history"), *Erzählung* ("story"), or *Satire*.

19. Alewyn, *Beer*, p. 49.

20. The German term *Gymnasium* has no adequate English translation. Perhaps the expression "preparatory school" comes closest. In the *Gymnasium* one learned, or rather continued to learn, Latin, rhetoric, Greek, mathematics, usually French, and in the more progressive schools, how one best "got along" in the real, political world.

21. The castle and church still stand, in apparently good condition.

22. See in this connection C. J. Opel, "Der Musenhof zu Weissenfels unter den Herzögen von Sachsen," *Blätter für Handel, Gewerbe und sociales Leben* 52 (1883):411.

23. *Diary*, p. 24.

24. We know little about the relationship between Beer and Krieger. The latter is mentioned only three times in Beer's diary, and here, as elsewhere, Beer disappoints us; he does not discuss Krieger as a musician or composer, nor does he go into their working relationship. We are left equally in the dark about his theories of the novel, and his relationship with Johannes Riemer, an important contemporary novelist who taught at the *Gymnasium* until 1687. The novels of Beer and Riemer bear close resemblances in many respects, and it is difficult to imagine that the two men did not, at some point, discuss the moral and aesthetic intentions of their works. One cannot exclude the possibility of their artistic collaboration in some of Beer's novels.

25. Erdmann Neumeister, *Specimen Dissertationis { . . . } de Poëtis Germanicis { . . . }* (Leipzig, 1695).

26. See Alewyn, *Beer*, p. 61.

27. See *Ursus murmurat*, p. A4^r. Reprinted in my introduction to the *Verliebten Oesterreicher*, p. 29.

28. *Diary*, p. 28.

29. Again, the word "novel" is used in the broadest sense. It would be more accurate to speak of works such as Beer's *Bestia Civitatis* as polemics or pasquinades.

30. See Helmut Krause, *Feder kontra Degen. Zur literarischen Vermittlung des bürgerlichen Weltbildes im Werk Johannes Riemers* (Berlin, 1979), pp. 57ff. Riemer received the protection of the Duke against the city council.

31. Beer, *Musicalische Discurse*, pp. 18f.

32. See Werner, *Städtische*, pp. 65f.

33. See Alewyn, *Beer*, pp. 52f. Recently Manfred Lischka provided a bibliography of Beer's musical works which corrects some errors in Alewyn. See *Daphnis* 9, Heft 3 (1980):557–96.

34. In the diary he mentions an offer from Coburg (pp. 26f) and even from the Royal Court in Denmark (p. 33, Schmiedecke ed.)

35. On the musical aspect of Beer's writings see Heinz Krause, *Johann Beer 1655—1700: Zur Musikauffassung im 17. Jahrhundert* (Saalfeld:1935). (Diss., Leipzig.)

36. There is considerable evidence, e.g., that he carried on a protracted feud with the composer and novelist Wolfgang Caspar Printz, an adherent of the musical theories of the Jesuit polyhistorian Athanasius Kircher, whom Beer attacked by name in his *Ursus Vulpinatur* (1697). Beer confined Printz to the eighth cell of his Fools' Asylum (*Narrenspital*) because of his musical views and apparently made light of him in the *Welt-Kucker*. Printz's printed response came out belatedly, to say the least, in 1745, in the odd work *Vertheidigung des löblichen Schneider-Handwercks*, at a time when a polemic against Beer was hardly timely. See H. K. Krausse's edition of the works of Printz (Berlin: De Gruyter, 1979), vol. 2.

37. "A man," as the renowned eleventh edition of the *Britannica* puts it, "of wide and varied learning but singularly devoid of judgment and critical discernment."

38. Quoted by Krause, *Beer*, pp. 70f.

39. Music written in the Dorian mode, to use the musical term. Little seems actually to be known about the practice of ancient Greek musicians.

40. Quoted by Krause, *Beer*, p. 72. See Krause for a detailed discussion of the Beer-Vockerodt feud as well as for a partial listing of Beer's compositions.

41. See Krause, *Beer*, p. 72.

42. Ibid., pp. 72—75.

43. See Arno Werner, "Beer," in: *Die Musik in Geschichte und Gegenwart: Allgemeine Enzyklopädie der Musik* (Kassel, 1949—51), 1:col. 1508.

44. See *Diary*, p. 42.

45. Ibid.

46. Ibid.

47. Ibid., pp. 48—55.

48. See Alewyn, *Beer*, pp. 144—47.

49. See *Diary*, pp. 59—61.

50. On the extravagances and entertainments at court see Werner, "Beer," pp. 54ff.

51. In a printed eulogy to the Duke it is reported that he not only furthered the arts, but also excelled in poetry and music. See Gerhardt, *Geschichte der Stadt Weissenfels a. S.* (Weissenfels, 1907), p. 230.

52. See Gerhardt, *Weissenfels*, pp. 228f.

53. *Diary*, p. 67.

54. Ibid., pp. 73, 77.

55. At the end of the novel *Der deutsche Kleider-Affe* of 1685 Beer renounces the writing of works "of that sort," but gives no reason for his decision. It is interesting that his contemporary Riemer ceased, for practical and possibly genuine religious reasons (he left Weissenfels and became a pastor in Oster-

wieck), to write novels at about the same time. Whatever his reason, Beer ceased to allow his novels to be published from 1685 until 1697. Another fascinating question is whether the three novels that appeared after 1697 were actually written much earlier, or whether they were written in Beer's last years, in which case they would presumably reflect the outlook of a much more experienced man. In this connection, see my "A Note on Johann Beer's *Der verkehrte Staats-Mann,*" *Daphnis* 4 (1975):202–4.

56. *Musicalische Discurse*, p. 177.

57. Garthoff survived and was still alive as late as 1726, although he lost his lower lip in the accident. See Jacob Adlung, *Anleitung zu der musikalischen Gelahrtheit* (Erfurt: Bach, 1785), footnote on page 99 (but not present in the second edition). Interesting but unfortunately vague is Adlung's remark that Beer in maturer years regretted having written his novels (see pp. 101–2). The account in the diary occurs on page 93.

58. The sermon was given by Johann Christoph Stange, professor of rhetoric at the Weissenfels *Gymnasium*. A copy exists in the Nationale Forschungs- und Gedenkstätten der klassischen Deutschen Literatur, Weimar.

Chapter Two

1. As Alewyn speculates. See Alewyn, *Beer*, pp. 236f.

2. On the *Amadís* in Germany see the thorough study by Hilkert Weddige, *Die "Historien vom Amadis auss Franckreich"* (Wiesbaden: Steiner, 1975).

3. See Alewyn, *Beer*, p. 268.

4. Ibid., pp. 266ff. Alewyn does not list all examples.

5. Ibid., p. 238; Manfred Kremer, *Die Satire bei Johann Beer* (Diss., Cologne; printed in Düsseldorf, 1964), pp. 67f.; Ilse Hartl, "Die Rittergeschichten Johannes Beers" Diss. Vienna, 1947; typewritten.

6. Portions of the section dealing with *Adimantus* appeared in my article "Johann Beers Parodie 'Printz Adimantus,'" *Akten des V. Internationalen Germanisten-Kongresses Cambridge 1975* (= *Jahrbuch für Internationale Germanistik*, Reihe A), 2/3: 82–89.

7. The name, probably by design, resembles that of Oriane, the beloved of Amadís de Gaula.

8. All quotations are taken from the easily accessible Reclam edition by Hans Pörnbacher (Stuttgart, 1967). Here the quotation is from p. 25.

9. Ibid., p. 29.

10. It is not known whether Beer knew French, and there is no evidence that he knew Dutch. See Alewyn, *Beer*, p. 146; Günther Weydt, *Nachahmung und Schöpfung im Barock* (Bern: Francke, 1968), pp. 146–51; Max Neumann, "Cervantes in Deutschland," *Die neueren Sprachen* 25 (1917):Teil I, 153–62; Teil II, 193f.

11. *Ursus vulpinatur* (Weissenfels, 1697).

12. Alewyn, *Beer*, p. 65.

13. See Ulrich Maché, "Die Überwindung des Amadisromans durch Andreas Heinrich Buchholtz," *Zeitschrift für Deutsche Philologie* 85 (1966):542−59, and Walter E. Schäfer, "Hinweg nun Amadis und Deinesgleichen Grillen!" *Germanisch-Romanische Monatsschrift*, N.F. 15 (1965):366−84.

14. See John J. O'Connor, *Amadis de Gaule and Its Influence on Elizabethan Literature* (New Brunswick, N.J.: Rutgers University Press, 1970): "Extremes of inflated language are rare" (p. 98). The *Amadís* was often attacked in the seventeenth century for its allegedly overadorned language, probably because its detractors accepted earlier condemnations uncritically and with no direct knowledge of the work.

15. "[. . .] Du wollest den Mist meiner Grobheit auf dem Schubkarn deiner Benevolentz in das Wasser der Vergessenheit führen [. . .]" (p. 9).

16. Windfuhr documents the seventeenth-century predilection for genitive constructions, e.g., *Schlafsucht der Faulheit* ("sleep-mania of indolence"), in Harsdörffer's *Gesprechspiele*, 1641−49. See Manfred Windfuhr, *Die barocke Bildlichkeit und ihre Kritiker* (Stuttgart: Metzler, 1966), p. 55.

17. *Adimantus*, p. 16.

18. One of his early detractors was Johann Rist, who refers to Zesen as *Sausewind* ("windbag") in *Das Friede wünschende Teütschland* (n.p., 1647).

19. *Jucundus Jucundissimus*, p. 197.

20. Ibid., p. 200.

21. *Corylo*, 1:200.

22. John Barclay (1582−1621), Scottish-French author of the Latin novel *Argenis* (1621), one of the most influential literary works in seventeenth-century Europe. Translated into German by Martin Opitz in 1626−31.

23. See Alewyn's edition, p. 339.

24. *Welt-Kucker*, 1:114.

25. Ibid., p. 117.

26. *Winternächte*, p. 63. All references to the *Winternächte* and *Sommertäge* come from the Alewyn edition (Frankfurt a.M.: Insel-Verlag, 1963).

27. *Winternächte*, pp. 79ff.

28. Alewyn, *Beer*, p. 135.

29. See Windfuhr, *Bildlichkeit*, p. 267. Birken was a poet and tutor to the Brunswick princes, including the novelist Duke Anton Ulrich von Braunschweig.

30. See *Ertz-Narren*, pp. 99, 100, 276ff. All citations come from the 1679 edition, *sine loco et anno*.

31. *Ertz-Narren*, pp. 113f.

Chapter Three

1. See in this connection Alexander A. Parker, *Literature and the Delinquent* (Edinburgh: Edinburgh University Press, 1967); Helmut Heidenreich, ed., *Pikarische Welt: Schriften zum europäischen Schelmenroman* (Darmstadt: Wissenschaftliche Buchgesellschaft, 1969).

2. Parker, *Delinquent*, p. 6.

3. Kenneth Negus has provided an excellent treatment of Grimmelshausen in the Twayne World Authors Series (New York: Twayne Publishers, 1974).

4. Hans. F. Menck sees in the *Welt-Kucker* the "first German musicians' novel." *Der Musiker im Roman* (Heidelberg: Winter, 1931), p. 9.

5. Eunuchs were probably in constant use as singers in Constantinople from the time the Eastern Empire was created until it fell. In the West, the *castrati* appear to have been victorious over soprano falsettists (not eunuchs), and were sanctioned by the Vatican to perform Church music—women were not allowed to sing in church until the seventeenth century—around 1625. From that time until the end of the eighteenth century *castrati* were a *sine qua non* for Italian opera. They were among the most celebrated artists of the age, and much in demand among women, for reasons that are not entirely transparent. See Angus Heriot, *The Castrati in Opera* (New York: Da Capo Press, 1974).

6. In this connection see Christian Stehr, "Johann Beers *Symplicianische Welt-Kucker:* Picaroroman—Verwildertes Experiment—Oder Literatursatire?" (Diss., University of Oregon, 1975).

7. See Stehr, "Beers *Welt-Kucker*," pp. 42–66.

8. K. G. Knight, "The Novels of Johann Beer," *Modern Language Review* 56 (1962):196.

9. "Das Dach war allenthalben offen, deswegen ging der Wind Tag und Nacht auf mich, und wenn es regnete, benetzte es mich, dass es taugte. Ich hatte einen kleinen Puffer, den musste mir der Schüler verkaufen, und um dasselbige Geld liess ich mir einige Bratwürste bringen, die frass ich in dem grössten Hunger in den Bauch hinein und trank Kovent dazu [. . .]. Zuweil kamen die rammelnden Katzen, die trieben ihr Spiel hinter und vor mir. Sie sprangen kreuzweise über mein Bette, und weil ich mich vor grosser Schwachheit kaum rühren konnte, kratzten sie mir Maul und Nase wund. Wenn ich meine Notdurft verrichten sollte, musste ich auf einen Dachziegel hofieren und solchen hinunter auf die Gasse werfen. [. . .] Nach dieser Krankheit durfte ich vierzehn Tage keine harte Arbeit mehr tun und wurde mit Bierholen, Holzhauen, Auskehren und dergleichen verschont, und weil ich wegen Schwachheit noch nicht zur Schule gehen konnte, musste ich indessen zuhause liegen und Gersten klauben, Äpfel schälen, Garn abhaspeln, die Kinder wiegen und dergleichen" (Alewyn edition, p. 105).

10. Pp. 140f. This and all other quotations from *Bruder Blau-Mantel* are taken from the facsimile edition by Manfred Kremer, which includes a very useful introduction and commentary. There was only one printing of the work. Kremer succeeded in locating the only known extant copy at the Bibliothèque Nationale et Universitaire in Strasbourg.

Chapter Four

1. I concur with Manfred Kremer's designation of almost half of Beer's novelistic production as "political" (Kremer, *Satire*, p. 31). Alewyn did not

grapple with the genre but classified as satires most of the novels we classify here as "political." Kremer states that Alewyn accepted without reservation his designation of ten novels as political in a letter of 1968 (cf. "Genesis," p. 76). V. Meid lists four Beer novels as political (Meid, *Barockroman*, p. 83); Huala, only three (*Der pol. Feuermäuerkehrer, Bratenwender, Die andere Ausfertigung*: see Waldemar Huala, "Die Romane Johann Riemers," (Diss., University of California, Los Angeles, 1975, pp. 112f.).

    2. Although the *Verkehrte Staats-Mann* appeared only in 1700, it is quite possible that it was written much earlier.

    3. See Arnold Hirsch, *Bürgertum und Barock im deutschen Roman* (Frankfurt, 1934; 2d ed. Cologne, 1957), pp. 40ff. Not all scholars agree with this thesis: cf. Kremer, "Zur Genesis des politischen Romans im 17. Jahrundert," *Akten des V. Internationalen Germanisten-Kongresses Cambridge 1975* (= *Jahrbuch für internationale Germanistik*) Reihe A, Heft 3 (Bern: Lang, 1976):74−81.

    4. Hans Wagener has treated Weise's novels in some detail in *The German Baroque Novel* (New York: Twayne Publishers, 1973), pp. 86−96, so that further discussion of their plots is unnecessary here. I am much indebted to Hans Arno Horn, *Christian Weise als Erneuerer des deutschen Gymnasiums im Zeitalter des Barock* (Weinheim: Beltz, 1966).

    5. In other countries the genre seems to be unknown.

    6. Niccoló Machiavelli's *Il Principe* (1513) is a justification of *Realpolitik*. Baldassare Castiglione, author of *Il Cortegiano* (1528), an immensely popular work that provided the aristocratic world with a portrayal of the ideal courtier, was a man imbued with chivalric virtues and humanistic learning. Baltasar Gracián y Morales was a Spanish priest and writer. His works treat in part the proper deportment of courtiers and the rules for the prudent conduct of one's life. His philosophical allegory *El Criticón* (1651) and *Oráculo Manual* (1647) were quite influential on Weise and on seventeenth-century German culture in general. See Rudolf Becker, *Christian Weises Romane und ihre Nachwirkung* (Diss., University of Berlin, 1910). Francisco Gómez de Quevedo y Villegas was a Spanish writer, author of the influential picaresque novel *El gran buscón* (1626) and of *Los sueños* (1627), a mordant satire on virtually every trade and profession. The work appeared in an important German adaptation by Moscherosch under the title *Gesichte Philanders von Sittewald* (1646). Traiano Boccalini was an Italian satirist, author of a learned and influential satire, *Ragguagli di Parnaso* [Relations from Parnassus, 1612], which was translated by the German Rosicrucian circle in 1617, and of *Pietra del Paragone* [The Politicke Touchstone, 1615]. The *Ragguagli* is a light, imaginative satire that attacks the actions and works of historical figures both contemporary and ancient including Seneca and Michelangelo. See P. Stötzner, "Der Satiriker Trajano Boccalini und sein Einfluss auf die deutsche Literatur," *Archiv für das Studium der neueren Sprachen und Litteraturen*, ser. 53, vol. 103 (1899). Francis Bacon was an English philosopher, Humanist, member of Parliament, founder of English empiricism, author of *Advancement of Learning* (1605), and *Novum Organum* (1620), both of which urge the inductive method.

7. Heinrich Zedler, *Universal-Lexikon* (Leipzig and Halle, 1741 ff.).

8. See Krause, *Feder kontra Degen.* Contrary to the statements of literary historians of the nineteenth and twentieth centuries, Riemer was no mere imitator of Weise. Krause argues convincingly that, while he used Weise's *Bericht* as a guide for the writing of his own political novels, the younger author was the more talented novelist. His skill lay in concealing the theoretical, "political" messages of his novels in a wealth of descriptive detail. Krause's study of Riemer is by far the most accurate, detailed and authoritative yet published. Of particular interest are the new details on Riemer's life and his relationship with the populace of Weissenfels.

9. See, e.g., his *Der gelehrte Redner* [The Learned Speaker, 1692].

10. Kuhnau's *Schmid seines eignen Unglückes* [Smith of His Own Misfortune, 1695], e.g., follows Weise's instructions in *Bericht* precisely, both as to structure and "message." Johann C. Ettner, a physician, wrote a novel in six parts between 1694 and 1715 that combines medical lore with political sagacity.

11. See Rolf Grimminger, "Roman," in: *Hansers Sozialgeschichte der deutschen Literatur vom 16. Jahrhundert bis zur Gegenwart*, ed. R. Grimminger, vol. 3: *Deutsche Aufklärung* (Munich: Hanser, 1980), p. 648.

12. These and the following remarks on the political novel are based in part on previously cited works by Alewyn, Kremer, Kirsch.

13. See Kremer, "Genesis," p. 74.

14. See H. Krause, *Feder*, pp. 370−71.

15. Kremer quite correctly points out that Alewyn's designation of these works as "satires" is not helpful since the term satire pertains to a basic attitude and not to formal-aesthetic criteria. Satire, in other words, is not a genre and certainly not a subgenre of literature.

16. See Kremer, *Satire*, pp. 81f.

17. As Kremer (*Satire*, pp. 80−85) has suggested.

18. Alewyn knew of the existence of this novel, but a copy was located only in 1959, in the Zentralbibliothek der deutschen Klassik, Weimar, by K. G. Knight.

19. It is no wonder that Beer's antifeminist novels were attacked by several contemporaries, including the anonymous author of the *Ausgekehrte politische Feuermäuer-Kehrer* [The Excoriated Political Chimney-Sweep], whose pique may have arisen more from Beer's muckraking in the sexual practices of Weissenfels than from broader cultural issues such as the portrayal of most women as gossips, slatterns, and viragoes.

20. See the concluding paragraphs of the *Jungfer-Hobel*.

21. See *Hansers Sozialgeschichte* 3:655ff.

22. Cf. Kremer, *Satire*, pp. 82−87.

23. Most of these epigrams were printed separately in 1691. Some appear in this collection in revised form.

24. The funeral sermon blossomed in the second half of the sixteenth century, reached a highpoint of popularity around 1670, and slowly declined until it died out toward the middle of the eighteenth century. This printed

funeral sermon was particularly widespread in the Lutheran lands of Germany, less so in Catholic and Calvinist areas. It is estimated that there are at least 100,000 extant funeral sermons of the period 1550—1700. They are extremely important for genealogical, medical, religious, and literary studies. See Eberhard Winkler, *Die Leichenpredigt im deutschen Luthertum bis Spener* (Munich: Kaiser, 1967), pp. 9—13.

25. Actually shawm, old double-reed instrument, predecessor of the oboe.

26. Quoted from Alewyn's reprint, *Das Narrenspital sowie Jucundi Jucundissimi* (Hamburg: Rowohlt, 1957). pp. 9—10.

27. Alewyn found a resemblance between Lorenz and Goncharov's famous figure, Oblomov; the comparison is not so farfetched as one might think. Cf. Alewyn's "Nachwort" to the reprint of *Narrenspital*, p. 150.

28. Alewyn reprint, p. 16.

29. I.e., circa 1400—1700, until recently perhaps the most neglected period in German literature.

30. Alewyn reprint, p. 17.

31. Ibid., p. 24.

32. Ibid.

33. Cf. *Bericht* (1680), pp. 110ff.

34. Alewyn reprint, p. 16.

35. The best-known examples of which, to be sure, appeared after publication of this novel.

36. See especially pp. 139—40.

37. See Helmut Krause, *Feder*, p. 411; and "Mutmassungen über Riemer: Zu Hans-Dieter Brackers Aufsatz 'Johann Riemers satirische Romane,'" *Daphnis* 6 (1977): 147—69. A. Hirsch first attributed the work to Beer: cf. Alewyn, *Beer*, p. 257, footnote 4.

38. In the prologue Beer mentions the fact that he lay seriously ill with a fever for several weeks while writing the novel and that he was assisted in completing it by a "friend." In Beer's *Diary*, we find an entry under April 1683 indicating he suffered from a ten-week fever contracted in Eisenberg; we may assume that the novel was completed in that time.

39. Pepys, e.g., paid £ 4 5s in 1660 for a beaver hat, a sum that was then almost equivalent to six months' wages for an experienced mason. On this and the other data on clothing see Walter Minchinton, "Patters and Structures of Demand 1500—1750," in: *The Fontana Economic History of Europe: The Sixteenth and Seventeenth Centuries* ed. C. M. Cipolla (Glasgow: Wm. Collins, 1st ed. 1974, 2d ed. 1976), pp. 108—34.

40. Quoted by Minchinton, "Patterns," p. 110.

41. "Das ist eben die listige Staats-Maxime eines Potentaten / dass er denen Völckern / so er unter sein Joch zu bringen trachtet / erstlich seine Sprache / Kleider-Trachten / und Landes-Sitten [. . .] beybringet / damit ihnen allgemach seine neue Herrschaft erträglicher und besser / als ihre eigene / scheinen möge" (pp. 87—88).

42. Johann Kuhnau, author of two extant novels, both of which are excellent

examples of the political genre. See my bibliography in *Daphnis* 10 (1981): 325—43.

43. "[. . .] Und ob ich es wohl vor ein geringes Glück schätzte / mich auffs neue in menschliche Gesellschafft einzulassen / so triebe mich doch die schuldige Barmhertzigkeit aus meiner Felssen-Klufft hervor [. . .]" (p. 8).

44. "[. . .] Wer ein wahrer Einsidler sein will / nicht so wohl die Menschen / als ihre Laster fliehen missen" (pp. 68f.).

45. He resembles Pardophir in the *Verliebte Oesterreicher* and an itinerant confidence man in the *Winternächte*.

46. "Sein Mantel bestunde aus Pergament. Seine Hosen von Lesch-Papier [. . .]" (p. 127).

47. "sie nur mit einer wiedrigen Mine angesehen wurden" (p. 133).

48. "Dass ihm ein grausam breites und hässliches Post Scriptum über die Nase hinge" (p. 133).

Chapter Five

1. There was evidently only one edition. A critical edition with commentary by James Hardin appeared in the series *Nachdrucke deutscher Literatur des 17. Jahrhunderts* (Bern: Peter Lang, 1978).

2. Particularly in the first fifty pages of the work.

3. "In solchen Gedancken satzte ich mich in einen Sessel / und ward von so vilen Liebs-Affecten fast schwerer / als ein Esel mit Mühl-Sacken beladen" (p. 148).

4. *Verliebte Oesterreicher*, pp. 20f. "Er wird vielmehr von einer guten Pfeiffe Toback / als einer klugen Hauss-Wirthschafft zu discuriren wissen. Die kirche besucht er nur aus Gewohnheit / und wo er nicht muss / sihet man ihn nimmermehr bey einer Messe."

5. Ibid., p. 182.

6. Ibid., pp. 246—47. "Tag und Nacht stackte ich in Sorgen / mein Gewissen war ohne Frieden / die Andacht ohne Ernst / das Hertz in steter Betrübnuss. Aber was ist dises alles anders / als ein Abbildung dess gantzen Menschlichen Lebens?"

7. The problem emerges at the very outset of the novels; cf. p. 17.

8. "Fressen / Sauffen und Schlaffen sind seine beste exercitien, die er die Zeit seines Lebens studirt / und die Meinung / dass das Geblüt allein den Adel bringe / hat ihn zu allen disen oberzehlten Untugenden geleitet" (p. 23). See also p. 198: noble birth without virtue and bravery is worthless.

9. *Verliebte Oesterreicher*, p. 41. "Mein Herr / diese Kunst haben wenig vom Adel studirt / dann er weiss wol / dass die Tugend alleine Edel mache / darum rede ich nicht von ihme als einem vom Adel / sondern lobe ihn als ein tugendsamen Menschen [. . .]."

10. *Die teutschen Winter-Nächte und Die kurzweiligen Sommer-Täge* (Frankfurt am Main: Insel-Verlag, 1963). Edited and with afterword by Richard Alewyn.

Since this reprint is widely available and copies of the original are extremely rare, all citations refer to the reprint.

11. See Edgar G. Knox. "Johann Beer's *Winternächte* and *Sommertäge*: Non-Courtly Elements in the German Novel of the Baroque Period" (Diss., University of Southern California, 1968).

12. Knox, "J. Beer's *Winternächte*, p. 10, gives four examples. Cf. also Alewyn's edition of the novels, pp. 867, 869.

13. There might be some truth in that statement since it is possible that Beer's *Winternächte* (henceforth *WN*) was influenced by Antonio de Eslavas's *Noches de Invierno* (Pamplona, 1609), which was translated into German by Matthäus Drummer in 1649. Jörg-Ulrich Fechner argues that such an influence is present, but his evidence is far from overwhelming. See Fechner, "Übersetzung, Nachahmung u. problematischer Einfluss. Eine komparatistische Fragestellung [. . .]," *Argenis* 2, Heft 1—4 (1978):73—94.

14. "Es war allgemach Mitternacht, als ich mich ganz ledig ausser dem Schloss befand, darinnen ich bis dahero mit tausend Sorgen und Grillen gefangen gessessen" (p. 12).

15. I take the word *Schinder* of the original to mean "skinner" rather than executioner or hangman, although it had the latter meaning in some seventeenth-century German dialect areas.

16. See Alewyn edition, p. 109.

17. Ibid., p. 422.

18. Ibid., p. 846.

19. Ibid., pp. 270f. "Ich habe mich in vielen Stücken selbst durchgezogen und unter andern Historien meine eigene Zustände entworfen. Habe also in diesen Winternächten in dem Schnee vorangewandelt, auf dass mir diejenige, so ich dort und da getroffen, desto leichter, gleichsam in einem gemachten Pfad, folgen möchten. [. . .] Die Ursach dieser Schrift ist nicht entsprossen aus einer eitlen Phantasie, sondern aus dem getanen Versprechen, dass ich alle diejenige Handlungen beschreiben wolle, welche mir und denjenigen, so bis dahin mit mir umgegangen, begegnet [. . .] Ich hätte zwar die Mühe solcher Schrift dem Herrn Irländer oder einem andern gerne gönnen wollen, aber weil sie mich hierzu gleichsam genötigt, hab ich um soviel desto bessere Ursach gehabt, die Sach also zu beschreiben, wie es an sich selbsten gewesen."

20. See Jörg-Jochen Müller, *Studien zu den Willenhag-Romanen Johann Beers* (Marburg, 1965), pp. 36ff.

21. Cf. Knox, "J. Beer's *Winternächte*," pp. 48ff.

22. Ibid., p. 49.

23. Alewyn edition, p. 140.

24. As claimed by Müller, *Studien*, p. 38.

25. Alewyn, edition, p. 270.

26. See Müller, *Studien*, pp. 39f.

27. Alewyn edition, p. 86.

28. As Müller has shown. Cf. *Studien*, pp. 60—65.

29. Not in 1668 as Müller unaccountably states. Cf. *Studien*, p. 61.

30. Beer refers incorrectly to "Eiselohn." Cf. Müller, *Studien*, p. 61.

31. Again, I am indebted to Müller's monograph for most of these data. Cf. *Studien*, pp. 63f.

32. Cf. Müller, *Studien*, pp. 65f.

33. The passage is written with care and clearly shows Beer's affection for his homeland. It occurs in the Alewyn edition on page 761 (Book V, Chapter XIX).

34. See Alewyn, *Beer*, pp. 196−203.

35. Ibid., p. 196. "Ein so reines und reiches Verhältnis zur Wirklichkeit ist im Barock keineswegs gewöhnlich, es unterscheidet Beer vielmehr völlig von allen zeitgenössischen und vorangegangenen Dichtern, vor allem von dem Phantasiemenschen Grimmelshausen."

36. See Alewyn, *Beer*, p. 197.

37. See, e.g., Hans Geulen, "Wirklichkeitsbegriff und Realismus in Grimmelshausens *Simplicissimus Teutsch*," *Argenis* 1 (1977):31−40. Geulen also makes the point that realism is not necessarily a constituent ingredient of the picaresque or "lower" novel in the seventeenth century any more than idealized situations are necessarily typical of the courtly novel. In a sense, Anton Ulrich's state novel *Octavia* (1677−1707, in six vols.) is more realistic than many picaresque novels. In short, realism should not be equated with genre.

38. See, e.g., Rolf Tarot, "Grimmelshausens Realismus." In: *Rezeption und Produktion zwischen 1570 und 1730. Festschrift für Günther Weydt zum 65. Geburtstag*. Ed. W. Rasch et al. (Bern and Munich, 1972), pp. 233−65. The article is enlightening, but its language, sometimes as dense and gnarled as one of Beer's forests, is a hindrance to comprehension.

39. Müller, *Studien*, p. 108.

40. In his *Diary* he writes: "Eine sehr grosse Thorheit ist es, die Gespänste leugnen" ("It's a very great foolishness to deny the existence of ghosts"), p. 152.

41. Alewyn edition, pp. 205−6. "Ich habe vor diesem in manchen Büchern ein Haufen Zeuges von hohen und grossen Liebesgeschichten gelesen, aber es waren solche Sachen, die sich nicht zutragen konnten noch mochten. War also dieselbe Zeit, die ich in Lesung solcher Schriften zugebracht, schon übel angewendet, weil es keine Gelegenheit gab, mich einer solchen Sache zu gebrauchen, die in demselben Buche begriffen war; aber dergleichen Historien, wie sie Monsieur Ludwigen in seiner Jugend begegnet, geschehen noch tausendfältig und absonderlich unter uns. Dahero halte ich solche viel höher als jene, weil sie uns begegnen können und wir also Gelegenheit haben, uns darinnen vorzustellen solche Lehren, die wir zu Fliehung der Laster anwenden und nützlich gebrauchen können."

42. Ibid., pp. 207−8.

43. Ibid., pp. 218−24.

44. Ibid., p. 11. "Ihr Freunde, die mir noch zum Trost und Freude leben, / Nehmt diese meine Schrift zu euren Diensten an. / Ich weiss euch anders nichts ᵃls dieses Buch zu geben, / Darin ihr mich und ich euch wiedersehen kann."

45. Alewyn edition, pp. 159f. "Wir glauben, dass Beer schwer unter seiner einfachen Geburt gelitten hat, und sehen in der Häufigkeit und der dichterischen Ausstattung dieses Motivs eine Bestätigung dafür" ("We believe that Beer suffered greatly from his humble birth and we see in the frequency and in the poetic treatment of this motif a confirmation of this").

46. Cf. Alewyn *Beer*, pp. 222f.

47. Alewyn edition, p. 86. "Auf eine solche Weise ging ich von dem Schloss hinweg und machte mir wunderseltsame Grillen. Ich wollte gern ein Finger aus der Hand darum geben, dass ich niemalen zu dieser Gesellschaft gekommen noch sie mit einem Auge gesehen hätte."

48. Alewyn edition, pp. 110f. "Ich hatte nur noch eine Schwester von fünfzehn Jahren, die war sehr tugendsam erzogen, dieselbe tröstete mich nach ihrem kindlichen Verstand und wusste nicht, wie sehr der Verlust desjenigen Dinges schmerze, welches man sowohl aus dem Besitz als der Hoffnung verloren. Der Vater selbst trauerte mit mir. Er weinete und stellete sich wegen meiner schmerzhafter, als ichs geglaubet hätte, dass ers sollte tun können. [. . .] Ich verschloss dannenhero das Zimmer und weinete ganz allein, ohne Trost und Hoffnung, wie der verlassenste Mensch unter der Sonnen."

49. Alewyn edition, p. 123. "Hiermit führte er mich mit sich über eine steinerne Treppe von acht Stufen hoch, daselbst setzte ich mich mit ihm in ein kleines Zimmer, allwo ich ihm ganz umständlich erzählet, wie und auf was Weise ich bis dahero gelebet und wie elend ich meine Zeit zugebracht hatte. Bald sprang er in die Höhe, bald setzte er sich wieder nieder, so sehr konnte er sich über meine Erzählung verändern. Er wand die Hände zusammen, schwang dieselbe bald über den Kopf, bald auf den Bauch, bald umfasste er mich mit beiden Armen und trieb ein rechtes Affenspiel mit mir."

50. Alewyn edition, p. 199.

51. Cf. Knox, "J. Beer's *Winternächte*," pp. 188ff.

52. Cf. Alewyn edition, p. 422.

53. Cf. Alewyn, *Beer*, pp. 233f.

54. As Alewyn states, ibid., p. 232.

55. Cf. Knox, "J. Beer's *Winternächte*," pp. 188ff.

56. Alewyn edition, p. 11. "Zu denen gehe hin, wo ich nicht hin kann gehen, / Mein Buch, und sprich, dass ich noch voller Flammen leb, / Auch, dass in solcher Glut mein Leben wird bestehen, / Bis ich der Eitelkeit mein letztes Vale geb.

57. Cf. Müller, *Studien*, pp. 102f.

58. On court cf. Alewyn edition, pp. 487ff; on praise of country life cf. Alewyn ed., pp. 453ff. Cf. also Knox, "J. Beer's *Winternächte*," pp. 196ff.

59. Alewyn edition, pp. 237−40. "Die satyrischen Schriften und andere Romanen gaben mir in allen Sachen das beste Licht, und ich achtete sie zu dem menschlichen Leben viel tauglicher und notwendiger als die Logik und alle andere Definitionen, weil ich gesehen, dass die Gelehrten viel uneiniger untereinander waren als die Satyri. [. . .] Aber ich bekenne es, dass ich daraus

zu einer bessern Beredsamkeit gekommen, als es mir mein Professor zwölf
Monat aneinander von der Stellung einer Oration dahergesagt hätte. [. . .]
Ich sah beinebenst, gleichsam als auf einem Theatro, wie es die Welt zu treiben
pfleget, und fand es nicht anders in dem Werke, als es mir der Buchstabe
gewiesen. Dadurch ward ich schon ein halber Politicus, denn es begeneten mir
viel Sachen, welche andern in dem Buche begegnet, und ich wickelte mich eben
durch diesen Vorteil heraus, durch welchen sie sich vorsichtig losgemachet.
[. . .] Denn die Definitionen taugten gar nicht in meinen Kram, und es ist
mir jetzt weit ein grösserer Nutze, dass ich weiss, wie und wann man das Feld
pflügen, das Korn säen, das Gras schneiden, die Äpfel abschütteln, die Schweine
in die Mast tun, die Kalber abnehmen, das Holz fällen, das Hausgesind regieren
und dergleichen nützliche Sachen tun solle, als wenn ich ein grosser Doctor
wäre. Und meine Scheunen prangen viel herrlicher angefüllet von Getreid als
mit Büchern. Dadurch lebe ich viel vergnügter in meiner Freiheit, welche ich
von Jugend auf so hoch gehalten, dass ich mich niemalen einer Meinung eines
Philosophi unterwerfen wollen."

    60. See Knox, "J. Beer's *Winternächte*," pp. 22f.

    61. There are limitations on the rights of the noblemen to punish those
charged of serious crimes, and a lawyer has to be consulted on legal matters.

Chapter Six

    1. Knight, "The Novels of Johann Beer (1655 – 1700)," p. 195.

    2. See note 57, Chapter 1.

    3. J. H. Scholte, *Der Simplicissimus und sein Dichter* (Tübingen: Niemeyer,
1950), p. 12.

    4. See Alewyn, *Beer*, p. 224, where he states he finds types, not individu-
als, in Beer's novels.

    5. Cf. *Winternächte*, Alewyn edition, p. 151.

    6. Ibid., pp. 226 – 27. "Viel hundert Paar gestrickte, zerrissene und
zerlumpte Strümpfe, die flickte ich mit meinem Schreibgezeug, und sie ver-
ehrten mir zum Recompens eine alte Paruque [. . .]. Meine Grammatica
zerriss ich in tausend kleinen Stücken, und dieselben Papierlein liess ich an
einem Spiesse braten und frass sie vor calecutische Hühnerfedern. Bald kam mir
eine mit Saiten bezogene Ofengabel vor das Bett, auf welcher ich länger als vier
Stunden aneinander musicieret. [. . .] Alle, die mich in dieser Krankheit
besuchten, hielt ich vor Felleisen, Flederwische, Turmknöpfe, Haselnüsse,
Schreibfedern, Bänkfüsse und auch Kuhschwänze [. . .]."

    7. Alewyn, *Beer*, p. 60f. "Verfasser der lustigsten und launigsten Bücher
seines Jahrhunderts."

Selected Bibliography

PRIMARY SOURCES

The author of this volume has provided a descriptive bibliography of all extant works by Johann Beer as well as a list of all known works and articles about Beer in volume 2 of the series *Bibliographien zur deutschen Barockliteratur* Bern and Munich: Francke, 1983.
1. Editions and Reprints
   A critical edition of the collected works of Johann Beer was announced some years ago by the de Gruyter publishing house. The project was dropped but was rescued by the Peter Lang Verlag, Bern, to be edited by Hans-Gert Roloff and Ferdinand van Ingen. In the meantime the following critical editions and reprints (some truncated) have appeared:
   A. Critical Editions
Der Simplicianische Welt-Kucker, ed. Hans-Gert Roloff and Ferdinand van Ingen. (Johann Beer. Sämtliche Werke vol. 1). Bern: Peter Lang, 1981. Not a fascimile edition. Includes textual variants found in the various editions of this work. The "Nachwort" elucidates Alewyn's position regarding the completion of the critical edition.
Der kurtzweilige Bruder Blau-Mantel. With an introduction and edited by Manfred K. Kremer. *Nachdrucke deutscher Literatur des 17. Jahrhunderts 29.* Bern, Frankfurt: Peter Lang, 1979. (Fascimile edition).
Der verliebte Österreicher. With an introduction, bibliography, and edited by James Hardin. *Nachdrucke deutscher Literatur des 17. Jahrhunderts 21.* Bern: Lang, 1978. (Fascimile edition).
   B. Reprints with Commentary, Unabbreviated
Die Geschicht und Histori von Land-Graff Ludwig dem Springer. Edited by Martin Bircher. Munich: Kösel, 1967.
Die kurtzweiligen Sommer-Täge. With an introduction and edited by Wolfgang Schmitt. Halle: VEB Max Niemeyer, 1958.
Das Narrenspital sowie Jucundi Jucundissimi Wunderliche Lebens-Beschreibung. With an introduction and edited by Richard Alewyn. Hamburg: Rowohlt, 1957.
Der neu ausgefertigte Jungfer-Hobel. Edited by Eberhard Haufe. Frankfurt am Main: Insel, 1968.
Printz Adimantus und der Königlichen Princessin Ormizella Liebes-Geschicht. Edited and with an afterword by Hans Pörnbacher. Stuttgart: Reclam, 1967.
Die teutschen Winter-Nächte und Die kurzweiligen Sommer-Täge. Edited and with an afterword by Richard Alewyn. Frankfurt am Main: Insel Verlag, 1963.
Der verkehrte Staats-Mann oder Nasen-weise Secretarius. Frankfurt am Main: Minerva GMBH, 1970. (No commentary provided.)

C. Abbreviated Reprints

Die Abenteuer des jungen Jan Rebhu. Edited by Josef Friedrich Fuchs. Vienna:
Amandus-Verlag, 1960. This is a "modernized" reprint of *Welt-Kucker* I
and was labeled volume 1 of the "collected works" of Johann Beer. Further
volumes did not appear.

Musicalische Discurse. Abbreviated reprint in: *Cäcilienkalender* 10(1885):61−75;
in the same periodical with the new title (since 1886) *Kirchenmusikalisches
Jahrbuch* 11 (1886):66−74; 12 (1887):82−88; 13 (1888):56−61; 14
(1889):72−83.

Die teutschen Winternächte. Edited and with notes by Carl Winkler. Erfurt:
Gebrüder Richter, 1943.

Der verliebte Österreicher oder Joannes Beer. A "biography" of Beer together with a
condensed version of his *Der verliebte Österreicher* and excerpts from other
novels by Beer. Edited and with commentary by Fritz Habeck. Graz:
Stiasny Verlag, 1961. Same work under the title *Johannes Beer: Der
verliebte Österreicher oder Kurtzweil mit Frauenzimmern* appeared in the same
location and with the same publisher in 1964.

Excerpts from the novels contained in anthologies are not included above.

2. The Chief Literary Works of Johann Beer
The long titles of the original works have of necessity been shortened
but always include the first words of the original title. Opera texts,
occasional poems, and works whose existence cannot be verified are not
included. Dates given are those of the first editions. A question mark
indicates that evidence as to publisher or place of publication is lacking
on the title-page of the work.

Des Abentheurlichen Jan Rebhu Spiridon aus Perusina. No place, no publisher
(Halle: Hübener?), 1679.

Des Abentheurlichen Jan Rebhu Artlicher Pokazi. No place, no publisher (Halle:
Hübener?), 1679.

Der Abentheuerliche, wunderbare, und unerhörte Ritter Hopffen-Sack. No place, no
date (Halle: Hübener, 1677).

Die Andere Ausfertigung Neu-gefangener Politischer Maul-Affen. No place, no
publisher (Leipzig: Weidmann?), 1683.

Des artlichen Pokazi Continuation oder Anderer Theil. No place, no publisher
(Halle: Hübener?)

Bellum Musicum Oder Musicalischer Krieg. No place, no publisher, 1701.

Der Berühmte Narren-Spital. No place, no publisher, 1681.

Des berühmten Spaniers Francisci Sambelle wolausgepolirte Weiber-Hächel. No place,
no publisher, 1680.

Das bittere Leyden und Sterben unsers Herren und Heylandes Jesu Christi. Weissenfels:
Brühl, 1695.

Der deutsche Kleider-Affe. Leipzig: Johann Friedrich Gleditsch, 1685.

Die Geschicht und Histori von Land-Graff Ludwig dem Springer aus Thüringen.
Weissenfels, 1698.

Johann Beerens { . . . } musicalische Discurse durch die Principia der Philosophie deducirt. Nuremberg: Peter Conrad Monath, 1719.

Johannis Beerii Austriaci, Serenissimi Principis Saxo-Weissenfelsensis Phonasci ac in Camera Musici, Deutsche Epigrammata. (German Epigrams.) Weissenfels: Brühl, 1691.

Jucundi Jucundissimi wunderliche Lebens-Beschreibung. No place, no publisher (Nuremberg: Hoffmann), 1680.

Der kurtzweilige Bruder Blau-Mantel. No place, no publisher, 1700.

Die mit kurtzen Umständen entworffene Bestia Civitatis. No place, no publisher, 1681.

Der neu ausgefertigte Jungfer-Hobel. No place, no publisher, 1681.

Der politische Bratenwender. Leipzig: Weidmann, 1682.

Der politische Feuermäuer-Kehrer. Strassburg (given on title page, but possibly only to mislead censors): Weidmann (Leipzig?), 1682.

Der symplicianische Welt-Kucker oder Abentheuerliche Jan Rebhu. Halle: Hübener, 1677.

Des simplicianischen Welt-Kuckers oder Abentheurlichen Jan Rebhu Anderer Theil. Halle: Hübener (?), 1678.

Des simplicianischen Welt-Kuckers oder Abentheuerlichen Jan Rebhu Dritter Theil. Halle: Hübener (?), 1679.

Welt-Kucker, 4. Teil; Halle, Hübener. (?), 1679.

Ursus murmurat. Weissenfels: Brühl, 1697.

Ursus vulpinatur. List wieder List, oder musicalische Fuchs-Jagdt. Weissenfels: [Brühl?] 1697.

Der verkehrte Staats-Mann oder Nasen-weise Secretarius. Halle: Zeidler & Musselius, 1700.

Der verliebte Europaeer oder wahrhafftige Liebes-Roman. Leipzig: Weidmann, 1682.

Der verliebte Österreicher. No place, no publisher (Nuremberg: Johann Hoffmann's widow and E. Streck?), 1704.

Die vollkommene comische Geschicht des Corylo. No place, no publisher (Nuremberg: Johann Hoffmann), 1679.

Zendorii á Zendoriis Teutsche Winternächte oder die ausführliche und denckwürdige Beschreibung seiner Lebens-Geschicht. No place, no publisher (Nuremberg: Hoffmann?), 1682.

3. Diary

Johann Beer: Sein Leben, von ihm selbst erzählt. Edited by Adolf Schmiedecke and with a foreword by Richard Alewyn. Göttingen: Vandenhoeck & Ruprecht, 1965. One of the few personal accounts of a German author of the seventeenth century. The list of persons at the end of the diary (provided by Schmiedecke) is incomplete.

4. Translations

There is none thus far in print. A translation of *Die kurtzweiligen Sommertäge* by G. P. Jordan and James Hardin is scheduled to appear in 1983 in the Peter Lang Verlag.

SECONDARY SOURCES

1. Beer as Musician and Courtier
Gerhardt, Friedrich. *Geschichte der Stadt Weissenfels a. S.* Weissenfels: R.
Schirdewahn, 1907, pp. 374ff.
————. *Schloss und Schloss-Kirche zu Weissenfels.* Weissenfels: Max Lehmstedt,
1898. Both works excellent sources of information.
Mattheson, Johann. *Grundlage einer Ehrenpforte, woran der Tüchtigsten Capell-
meister, Componisten, Musikgelehrten, Tonkünstler etc. Leben, Wercke, Verdienste
etc. erscheinen sollen.* Hamburg: 1740. Reprint Berlin: Leo Liepmannssohn,
1910. Mattheson was the first "biographer" of Beer and the source for most
later articles about him in the later lexicons.
Stange, Johann Christoph. *Das unversehene, aber doch Seelige Ende { . . . }
Herren Johann Bährs.* (Sermon on the occasion of Beer's funeral.) Weissenfels: Brühls Wittbe, 1700. A copy exists in the Nationalen Forschungs-
und Gedenkstätten der klassischen deutschen Literatur, Weimar. See also
Zeitschrift für Musikwissenschaft 13 (1930):46ff.
Werner, Arno. *Städtische und fürstliche Musikpflege in Weissenfels bis zum Ende
des 18. Jahrhunderts.* Leipzig: Breitkopf & Härtel, 1911. Rich in data
on the period and its music.

2. Beer as Writer
Alewyn, Richard. *Johann Beer. Studien zum Roman des 17. Jahrhunderts. Palaes-
tra* 181. Leipzig: Mayer & Müller, 1932. This epoch-making work
proved Beer to be the writer of at least eighteen novels previously attributed to pseudonymous or actual writers other than Beer. It is a fine combina-
tion of erudition, detective work, and good writing.
Bircher, Martin. "Neue Quellen zu Johann Beers Biographie." *Zeitschrift für
deutsches Altertum und deutsche Literatur* 100 (1971):230−42. New, signifi-
cant biographical data.
Habeck, Fritz. "Der verliebte Österreicher oder Johannes Beer." In his *In
eigenem Auftrag.* Selected and introduced by Wolfgang Kraus. (*Stiasny-
Bücherei*, Bd. 120) Graz und Wien: Stiasny Verlag, 1963, pp. 115−23.
Folksy but informative.
Hardin, James. "Johann Beers Parodie *Printz Adimantus.*" In: Akten des V.
Internationalen Germanisten-Kongresses Cambridge 1975. (*Jahrbuch für
Internationale Germanistik*, Reihe A). Bern: H. Lang, 1976, pp. 82−89.
Analyzes Beer's literary parody.
————. "A Note on Johann Beer's *Der verkehrte Staats-Mann.*" *Daphnis:
Zeitschrift für Mittlere Deutsche Literatur* 4, Heft 2 (1975):202−4.
Hirsch, Arnold. "Barockroman und Aufklärungsroman." *Etudes Germaniques*
9 (1954):97−111.
————. *Bürgertum und Barock im deutschen Roman.* 1st ed. Frankfurt am
Main, 1934; 2d ed. by H. Singer. Cologne and Graz: Böhlau, 1957. A

quite significant work on the development of the German novel in the late seventeenth century. Unfortunately long out of print.

Knight, K. G. "The Novels of Johann Beer (1655 – 1700)." *Modern Language Review* 56 (1962):194 – 211. A very good overview.

Krause, Helmut. *Feder kontra Degen. Zur literarischen Vermittlung des bürgerlichen Weltbildes im Werk Johannes Riemers.* Berlin: Hofgarten Verlag, 1979, pp. 23f., 65f., 328, 368, 410f., 415f., 435, 446f.

Kremer, Manfred. "Johann Beers *Bruder Blaumantel.*" *Neophilologus* 51 (1967): 392 – 95.

———. "Der Kantor im Werke Johann Beers." *Modern Language Notes* 88 (1973):1023 – 29.

Meid, Volker. *Der deutsche Barockroman.* Stuttgart: Metzler, 1974. (Sammlung Metzler vol. 128.) A handy introduction to Beer's place in the overall German literary scene, and useful to an understanding of the various subgenres of the novel at the end of the century.

Müller, Jörg-Jochen. *Studien zu den Willenhag-Romanen Johann Beers.* (*Marburger Beiträge zur Germanistik* 9.) Marburg: N. G. Elwert, 1965. Indispensable work for an understanding of the *Winter Nights* and *Summer Tales.*

Salmen, Walter, ed. *Der Sozialstatus des Berufsmusikers vom 17. bis 19. Jahrhundert.* Kassel: Bärenreiter Verlag, 1971.

Schoolfield, George C. *The Figure of the Musician in German Literature.* (*University of North Carolina Studies in the Germanic Languages and Literatures*, no. 19.) Chapel Hill: University of North Carolina Press, 1956, pp. 2, 197.

Tarot, Rolf. "Grimmelshausens Realismus." In: *Rezeption und Produktion zwischen 1570 und 1730. Festschrift für Günther Weydt zum 65. Geburtstag.* Edited by Wolfdietrich Rasch, Hans Geulen, and Klaus Haberkamm. Bern and München: Francke, 1972, pp. 233 – 65.

Wagener, Hans. *The German Baroque Novel.* (Twayne's World Authors Series, 229) New York: Twayne Publishers, 1973, pp. 67 – 79. A quite useful overview.

Weddige, Hilkert. *Die "Historien vom Amadis auss Frankreich": Dokumentarische Grundlegung zur Entstehung und Rezeption.* Wiesbaden: Franz Steiner, 1975. (*Beiträge zur Literatur des XV. bis XVIII. Jahrhunderts*, Bd. 2.) pp. 224ff., 233.

Weil, Hans Hartmut. "The Conception of Friendship in German Baroque Literature." *German Life and Letters* 13 (1959 – 60): 106 – 15.

Werner, Arno. "Johann Beer." In: *Die Musik in Geschichte und Gegenwart: Allgemeine Enzyklopädie der Musik.* Kassel: Bärenreiter Verlag, 1949 – 51, 1:cols. 1506 – 8.

Weydt, Günther. "Der deutsche Roman von der Renaissance [. . .] bis zu Goethes Tod." In: *Deutsche Philologie im Aufriss.* 2d ed. edited by W. Stammler. Berlin: Erich Schmidt, 1960, 2:cols. 1217 – 1356; on Beer, cols. 1257 – 59. Puts Beer in the broader context of the German novel of the late seventeenth century.

Wichert, Hildegard E. *Johann Balthasar Schupp and the Baroque Satire in*

Germany. (Columbia University Germanic Series, 22.) New York: King's Crown Press, 1952. Very informative and many references to Beer.

3. Dissertations

Hartl, Ilse. "Die Rittergeschichten Johannes Beers." Diss., Vienna, 1947.

Hofacker, Erich P., Jr. "The Transition from Baroque to Enlightenment in Johann Beer's Treatment of the Aristocrat." Diss., University of North Carolina, 1967.

Knox, Edgar Guerin. "Johann Beer's 'Winternächte' und 'Sommertäge': Non-courtly Elements in the German Novel of the Baroque Period." Diss., University of Southern California, 1968.

Krause, Heinz. *Johann Beer 1655—1700: Zur Musikauffassung im 17. Jahrhundert.* Diss., Leipzig, 1935. Saalfeld: Günthers Buchdruckerei, 1935.

Kremer, Manfred. *Die Satire bei Johann Beer.* Diss., Cologne, 1964. Düsseldorf: Rudolf Stehle, 1964. An important treatment of Beer's satirical novels.

Seitz, Johann. "Die Frau und ihre Stellung im Werk Johann Beers." Diss., University of Minnesota, 1971.

Snyder, Verne. "Aspects of the Grotesque in the Novels of Johann Beer." Diss., State University of New York at Buffalo, 1975.

Stehr, Christian Peter. "Johann Beers *Symplicianischer Welt-Kucker:* Picaroroman—verwildertes Experiment—oder Literatursatire?" Diss., University of Oregon, 1975.

Index